Jerusalem

Jerusalem

Arab Social Life, Traditions, and Everyday
Pleasures in the 20th Century

by Subhi S. Ghosheh
abridged and translated by Bassam Abou Ghazalah
foreword by Salma Khadra Jayyusi

OLIVE
BRANCH
PRESS

An imprint of Interlink Publishing Group, Inc.
www.interlinkbooks.com

First published in 2013 by

OLIVE BRANCH PRESS
An imprint of Interlink Publishing Group, Inc.
46 Crosby Street, Northampton, MA 01060
www.interlinkbooks.com

Original Arabic copyright © Subhi S. Ghosheh, 2013
English translation and foreword copyright © Salma Khadra Jayyusi, 2013
Design copyright © Interlink Publishing, 2013

Library of Congress Cataloging-in-Publication Data

Ghosheh, Subhi S.
Jerusalem : Arab social life, traditions, and everyday pleasures in the
20th century / by Subhi S. Ghosheh.
p. cm.
ISBN 978-1-56656-788-6 (pbk.)
1. Palestinian Arabs—Jerusalem—Social life and customs—20th century.
2. Muslims—Jerusalem—Social life and customs—20th century.
3. Jerusalem—Social life and customs—20th century. 4. Arab-Israeli conflict.
I. Title.
DS109.93.G48 2009   305.892'740569442—dc22   2009031629

Cover photo "Bread seller in Jerusalem" © Pavel Bernshtam | Dreamstime.com
Photos:
pp iii, 45, 46 courtesy of Library of Congress
pp vi, 2, 25, 36, 56, 66, 104, 116, 124, 142, 150, 158 courtesy of Subhi Ghosheh

This English translation is published with the cooperation of PROTA (Project of Translation from Arabic), founded and directed by Dr. Salma Khadra Jayyusi.

Printed and bound in the United States of America

To request our free 48-page catalog, please call us toll-free
at 1-800-238-LINK, visit our website at www.interlinkbooks.com,
or send us an e-mail at info@interlinkbooks.com.

Foreword vii
Preface ix

PART ONE 1
1. When Jerusalem Speaks 3
2. The Advent of Life 15
3. A New Family 25
4. A Delightful Wedding Night (*huna*) 37
5. Our Children, Our Souls 47
6. Learning is Enlightening 57

PART TWO 65
7. Religions 67

PART THREE 103
8. Play, Pleasure, and Love 105
9. Evenings of Pleasure 117
10. Festivals and Popular Occasions 125
11. Economic Traditions 133
12. The Permanent Jerusalem Carnival 143
13. The Tower of Babylon 147
14. Folk Medicine 151
15. Food and Cuisine 159
16. Death 171

Conclusion 181
Notes 183
Glossary 184

Dr. Subhi Ghosheh

Foreword

DR. SUBHI GHOSHEH'S NEW BOOK, *Jerusalem: Arab Social Life, Traditions, and Everyday Pleasures in the 20th Century*, is a welcome addition to the Jerusalem Book Library. A Jerusalemite himself, Dr. Ghosheh writes with the expertise of a native son. Born and raised in Jerusalem's Sheikh Jarrah Quarter, just outside the walls, he has witnessed and participated in all its social customs and occasions. As an adult, Dr. Ghosheh has experienced incarceration by the Israelis because of his activity defending his native city as it was being taken over by an occupying power armed to the teeth. Later on, when he was living as an expatriate in other parts of the Arab world, Jerusalem and what befell it year after year, remained vitally alive in his heart and mind. He wrote two books about his Jerusalem experience; the first, *Our Sun Will Never Set*, was published in 1986 and the second, *The Sun from the High Window*, on his experience in prison, was published in 1989. After the mass exodus of the Palestinians from Kuwait, instigated by the Iraqi invasion, he came to live in Jordan. There he founded the Jerusalem Day Committee, which has been active in the service of Jerusalem's history and present status ever since.

In this book, the author has depicted a wide range of Jerusalem's social norms, beliefs, and customs, many of them centuries old. He speaks of an Arab city in which Muslims, Christians, and Jews have lived together for centuries in amity and cooperation, but also of a city which has now fallen prey to a process of acquisition and control by Israelis; where many of its inherited historical aspects have been or are in the process of being transformed, with impunity, under the eyes and ears of the world.

This book was first made possible by the generous support of His Royal Highness, Prince Salman bin Abd al-Aziz, the Governor of the District of Riyadh. However, Dr. Ghosheh, in his enthusiasm to record as much as possible of his city's social history, came up with three volumes of work, which had to be contracted and translated to comply with PROTA's publication program on the city. To help out with this, the King Abd al-Aziz Public Library, represented by its Secretary General, Ustadh Faisal al-Mu'ammar, came again to our aid. For other publication concerns I used the donation to the city's library given to us by the Palestinian businessman and philanthropist, Mr. Salman Abbasi, originally from Silwan, the Jerusalem suburb now taken over by the Israelis and considerably transformed. I owe these donors my deepest thanks.

Many thanks are due to Dr. Subhi Ghosheh himself who, despite his numerous commitments as doctor and as the Director of the Jerusalem Day Committee, took the time to honor my request for a much needed book on this particular subject, and did his research and writing with great enthusiasm. Thanks are also due to Dr. Bassam Abu Ghazaleh who contracted this originally large book and translated it with meticulous care. Thanks to Dr. Elizabeth Hodgkin, historian and human rights activist, who has helped in the editing process of this book and checked its historical data. Many thanks are also due to Mrs. Hana Husseini Jufali for much needed last minute help.

Salma Khadra Jayyusi
Director, East-West Nexus/PROTA

Preface

WRITING COMPREHENSIVELY ABOUT JERUSALEM is not an easy job. It is a vital duty, however, to give this jewel of the world the historical, cultural, religious, human, and traditional importance it deserves.

Professor Salma Khadra Jayyusi, the scholar who has dedicated her life and knowledge to the task of enlightening the world about the greatness of the Arab and Islamic culture, has honored me with her request to write about Jerusalem, the habits and traditions of its people. Jerusalem is my beloved city, where I was born and brought up, and for which cause I have consecrated my life-long struggle.

Needless to say, hundreds of books have been written about Jerusalem, for it is a city that has an intimate relationship with the whole world. It is the city of feasts and festivals, and of religious rituals that are supposed to represent the pure spirit of humankind. Yet, it is a city of unique grief, a city that has been the target of conquerors more than twenty times. Still, it is the city that has always been the victor in the end.

Today, Jerusalem is suffering from an Israeli colonial invasion that first resulted in its partial occupation in May 1948, and in the capture of the rest of it in June 1967. Unjustly declared the eternal capital of Israel, its indigenous Arab identity, both Islamic and Christian, is being obliterated.

It is well known that many countries are eager to have not only some kind of representation in Jerusalem, but also some kind of hegemony over it. The late Jabra Ibrahim Jabra, the renowned Palestinian writer and artist, emphasized how many nations wished to have even a charity house in Jerusalem, a mosque or a church, be it small or big. Behind the thick walls of such places there are worlds of special environments, languages, arts, and music.

Each invader has reconstructed the history of Jerusalem to suit their needs. The Israelis, however, were not satisfied with this; they are swallowing the whole of Jerusalem on the grounds of a historical past which denies any history other than historical Judaism. Preferring to leave the historical facts and fabrications to specialized historians, I quote K.W. Whitelam's words that "ancient Israelite history is the domain of Religion or Theology and not of History."[1] In finding historical events, historiography today does not depend on court historians whose job is to write what may please the ruler. The Crusaders, for example, had claimed that the purpose of their campaign was to save Jerusalem from both the Muslim and Christian Arabs, the latter being members of the Greek Orthodox church, while Arab historians related a totally different story. This is comparable to the claim of European invaders of the Americas that they came peacefully to spread Christianity when they, in fact, committed great atrocities against the indigenous peoples.

We are left with the history of people's traditions and folklore to which historians give great importance in historiography. Tradition, according to Dr. Ghali Shukri, is a continuous stream of blood that, consciously or unconsciously, runs in our arteries. It is the collection of a nation's material and moral history since ancient times. Tradition, therefore, is a description of the norms and manners of societies in their continuous daily life. It is a living entity that is inherited from the foremothers and forefathers and passed on to the offspring with whom it grows and becomes deeply rooted. It reveals itself in the social relations between people, cuisine, styles of dress and furniture, as well as architecture.

The material inheritance of Jerusalem is its old architecture, which reflected the traditional way of life of the indigenous people within it. Jerusalem includes hundreds of historical monuments, mosques, churches, and graves, including those of many famous people. It includes the ancient *souq* (marketplace) with its unique architecture, sometimes crude but also sophisticated and subtle.

The various traditional handicrafts unique to Jerusalem derive their character from locally available raw material. When the Israelis occupied Palestine they exerted every effort to obliterate the traditional handicrafts of the country, as a way to obliterate Palestinian history at the same time. Sometimes they claimed these traditions as theirs, forgetting the fact that they had come from Europe, and had nothing to do with the local folklore of Palestine, which was an intrinsic part of Arab folklore. Palestinians and the rest of the world have lost the ancient buildings of the Old City that have been pulled down by the occupation authorities with the purpose of changing the old inherited character of the city. A blatant example is the destruction of the Moroccan Quarter in the Old City. The occupiers have changed the Arab names of the streets, and teach their students a doctored version of the history of Jerusalem in particular, and of Palestine in general. One of the bizarre rules that the occupation authorities have imposed is forbidding the harvest of some medical herbs, like thyme, which grows naturally in the mountains and has for a long time been part of the traditional foods of Palestinians. High taxes have been imposed on the handicrafts that have long been attractions for tourists visiting the Holy Land.

It is well known that every society has a stereotype personality that bears its unique character. A child of that society will subconsciously absorb the character of that personality. The traditions, habits, beliefs, and mythologies, which are generally called folklore, are what differentiate one people from another.

Our tradition, much affected by its different religious backgrounds, has a national identity that goes back deeply into our past. No matter how long our diaspora remains or how strong the efforts exerted by our oppressors to obliterate our character, this national identity must not be forgotten. Our duty here is to show actual facts to the world when Zionists try to distort the city's long history. We must not forget, also, our intellectual traditions which the Zionists try to obliterate through the syllabus given to Arab pupils at school or which are lost through the adoption of superficial western customs.

Recording our traditions and folklore is a way to pass them on to our younger generations who, because of the Israeli occupation, have not been fully exposed to them. The Israeli occupation of Palestine is trying hard to annul our traditions, and our duty is to stand strong in defending them. This is the purpose of my book, which is dedicated to giving a detailed picture of our popular traditions in Jerusalem, traditions that are similar in the whole of Palestine. This work also has the purpose of providing Palestinians who have been forced to leave their country with a link to their motherland, its traditions, and folklore. Palestine is a bridge that has never been destroyed by the many armies that have conquered the region.

Although conquerors could never settle in Palestine, this influx of people left a few who settled and were absorbed into the culture of Palestine, bringing with them their habits and traditions. In his research, Dr. Fuad Kanaan noticed that most Palestinian traditions were not purely Palestinian, but had roots in the rest of the Islamic world, especially with regard to music, marital traditions, and religious beliefs. Similarity with the Syrian, Lebanese, and Jordanian traditions is particularly obvious. Such traditions, according to Dr. Kanaan, go back thousands of years in history.

Jerusalem is in danger, and we must rescue it by going back to the roots of our traditions and the civilization that has kept our people together through thousands of years. Rebuilding the character of our people requires the revival of our traditions. In fact, we have a lot to learn from these traditions, be it material, intellectual, or spiritual.

In a statement published by the *Sunday Times* on June 15, 1969, Golda Meir, the late Israeli prime minister, said: "There is no such thing as a Palestinian people... It is not as if we came and threw them out and took their country. They didn't exist."

Such a statement shows how formidable the Israeli machine is that intends to obliterate our traditions and history. However, this evil machine has been too weak to have an effect on our people, especially on the present Palestinian generation. Still, one must be apprehensive regarding the forthcoming generations, and this strongly prompts us to acquaint them with their traditions and heritage. Recording our traditions is supposed to preserve them and preserve our national identity. For it represents the strong roots that go deep into our history and keeps the vital and warm relationship between our people and our homeland.

The citizen of Jerusalem personifies his traditions every moment of his life. Our folklore is perhaps the most important side of our life; it is a major support of our national culture. We, therefore, are bound to study it, record it, and spread it among the new generation and pass it on to the generations to come. Folklore, by a widely accepted definition, is the sum of beliefs, myths, traditional habits, common sayings, and popular songs and dances that have been passed from one generation to another. In the Palestinian case, preserving and sticking to our folklore is indeed a national and religious duty, for it is a spiritual means of defending our precarious existence, which is being endangered by Israeli rule. It is also a cultural means for the Palestinians in diaspora to have an intimate relationship with the homeland they were forced to leave. We should not be swept away by modernization on account of our traditions, nor overawed by western civilization and become like a tree that had lost its roots.

As adherence to our traditions should be practiced by intellectual and practical activity, this work will tell the reader about the social life of the people of Jerusalem in the 20th century and its relationship with ancient Canaanite traditions inherited over the centuries. Although it is true that some of the old habits and beliefs are in contradiction with modern science, the adherence of the majority of our people to them is a matter of continuity, not ignorance. In fact, the same thing happens in Europe, where people have been celebrating certain historical events in the same way their ancestors did.

I am indebted to Mrs. Hala al-Bitar al-Nashef for her great effort in revising this work and giving her invaluable suggestions. My thanks are also due to Prof. Salma Khadra Jayyusi who honored me with being involved in her distinguished cultural project. I am grateful to Mr. Mahfouz Jaber and his colleagues of the Information Centre at the Jerusalem Day Committee, in Amman, Jordan, for allowing me to use the valuable documents in their library. The same gratitude goes to Miss Amani Saif and Miss Sara Sadeq Abdulqader for their effort in typing the Arabic version of this work. Special gratitude goes to Mr. Farouq Zadeh for revising the study.

Writing this work has filled me with great pleasure, as it has given me the chance to research some facts about Jerusalem to which I had never had the chance to pay due attention. It also took me back to the beloved atmosphere of my life in Jerusalem, my home town from which I was deported by force. I do hope that I have been successful in serving the city I love, as well as its heroic people who have been kidnapped by a long and savage occupation and are looking forward to the time when they can regain their freedom.

PART ONE

Top: Bread, eggs, and falafel seller
Bottom left: Shoe shine stand
Bottom right: Juice vendor

1.
When Jerusalem Speaks

THIS SACRED PLACE CALLED JERUSALEM is not merely a piece of land with ancient houses and narrow lanes. It is a spiritual bond that links together two billion believers. Behind every stone green with algae in its historic paths is a sleeping memory and a multi-faceted discourse. At every corner of every alley in Jerusalem dwells the distant past. One can almost hear a soft voice from its ancient stones saying, "I am the strongest, I have no history, for I am the history of human life!"

Hundreds of books have been written on Jerusalem, showing its prime importance among the cities of the world and telling about its sacred Islamic, Christian, and Jewish places, as well as its kings and rulers. The noble city of Jerusalem has always been a spiritual lighthouse except when occupiers attacked its universality, culminating in recent times by the Zionist occupation and its exclusive strategy. Strong and eager, however, the city is still looking for the moment when it will gain its freedom once again.

Indeed, not by virtue of its ancient wall, but by virtue of the intimate relationship among its inhabitants and the remarkable coexistence between its Muslims, Christians, and Jews, Jerusalem has always been a fortress which is both strong and joyful. Arab Jews have never been persecuted the way other Jews in the non-Arab world have. Social cooperation, thanks to Islamic ethics, has always been the prominent character in the region. Many factors have helped to bring about this intimate social relationship among the people of Jerusalem, the most important of which are geographic, demographic, religious, and national.

Looking at the Old City of Jerusalem from the sky, one would think that it was composed of a single giant house. This is because almost all the houses are connected together, having common walls with their roofs overlooking each other. This interconnectedness made it possible for the revolutionaries against the British occupying army to hide and move freely from one house to another by jumping from one roof to the next. Narrow and paved with cobblestones, most of its lanes have arches surmounted by apartments. The lanes branch off into small neighborhoods or quarters that end with a narrow alley leading to a dead end called a *hawsh* (courtyard), around which families live.

The relationship between the various quarters was intimate, as their inhabitants would have many things in common, particularly their performance of religious rituals.

For every quarter there was a chief, called *mukhtar*, who carried a personal seal that he used in all documents signed by him. This post was actually inherited, but subject to the approval of the local governor. When the old *mukhtar* died, a group of the inhabitants of the quarter chose a new one and sent a note to the local governor for his official approval. Should the governor receive more than one request for *mukhtar*, he would have the right to decide which one was to be appointed. As people used to associate such *mukhtars* with the government in power, so for political reasons, the *muhktars* lacked popularity. They were accused of telling the authorities of the whereabouts of wanted people and of taking part in rigging elections. Still, people had to resort to them for mediation with the authorities. Until recently, the *mukhtar* was responsible for reporting cases of marriage, birth, and death, and obtaining certificates related to them. He also reported new inhabitants to the quarter, as well as those who left it.

Since houses were attached to each other, relationships among neighbors were intimate, for neighbors in Islamic and Arab traditions have always been respected. One of the prophetic traditions (*hadith*) says: "You are not a believer if you go to bed with a full stomach while you know that your neighbor is hungry." Old sayings in Arabic have the same theme. An example is one that says, "A neighbor nearby is more important than a brother far off." Another goes like this: "Before choosing your house, choose your neighbor." In fact, neighbors, on all occasions, behave with each other as if they were family. When a new family comes to live in the quarter, neighbors invite them for a lunch or supper, which is later reciprocated by the new family. This way, people get to know and befriend each other. One of the factors for creating this intimate relationship among neighbors was that, in the old days, the city lanes were not lit at night, and in the darkness movement from one place to another was difficult. On occasions like *'aza* (ceremonies of condolences) or weddings, neighbors would wholeheartedly offer their houses as venues.

The house had a special importance in the life of a Palestinian. It represented a place of privacy and protection, and of shared memories with those who were born and brought up there. Most houses, whether in the old or new city, had been inherited by the owners from their forefathers. Therefore, every house had its own historical record that families were keen to preserve. The Jerusalem poet, Kamal Dajani, expressed this in the following words:

> My house
> Which is that of my father and grandfather,
> Is my most precious property on earth.

Building a new house, together with marriages and the birth of a boy, were the most important occasions for celebration. When the roof of a new house was completed, the owners would invite their relatives and friends for a meal and the guests would bring useful gifts for their hosts. For technical and traditional reasons, the dome was an important part of the old building style. Most houses were of one story, as building over the dome was impossible. Later, however, this problem was overcome.

The mortar used in building was a mixture of lime, sand, and ashes in equal proportions. In addition to its use in covering and bleaching the walls and domes of the houses, it was also used in bleaching water wells. Buildings in the new city, however, followed the modern style. When the first stone of a building was laid, an important ritual was to slay a sheep, an action called "the foundation sacrifice," as an offer to appease the spirits that were thought to be dwelling in the house. The same would be done when the dome was completed. On both occasions, a Muslim sheikh or a Christian priest was called to perform a prayer of thanks. The meat of the sacrificed sheep was given away to the poor, and some people would stain their hands with the sheep's blood and print them on the front wall to repel demons.

Neighbors of different religions—Muslims, Christians, and Jews—lived peacefully together and shared the same customs. Jews coming from Europe, who lived in Arab rented houses, were usually poor and help was extended to them. Muslims and Christians in Jerusalem and other Palestinian towns lived together in total harmony. It was only when the British occupied Jerusalem and the rest of the country after World War One that the city was intentionally divided into four quarters: Islamic, Christian, Armenian, and Jewish. Still, this division did not separate people from each other. The avowed purpose was to create a balance among the various religions and sects. But the principle of "divide and rule" should not be forgotten here. In addition, the various quarters were mostly named after the major families that occupied them, and the markets were named according to the merchandise sold, like the meat market and the vegetable market.

Some of the old houses, as mentioned above, were on both sides of an alley (*ziqaq*), which was with or without a roof. This cluster of houses together with the alley was called *hawsh*. Roofed alleys were dark even during the daytime, and before the introduction of electricity in 1936, people carried lanterns with them, for street lights were put only in the main streets. Staircases were everywhere in the Old City and, when the stairs were many, they were called '*aqaba*, an Arabic word meaning an obstacle, for they were considered obstacles on the road. Arches over alleys were commonplace.

Houses of the Old City were architecturally similar in style and function. The main entrance was small with a gate made of iron or fortified wood. The door lock was large with an equally large and heavy key that made more than one turn in the lock for better protection. It is worth mentioning that most people who were forced to leave their houses after the 1948 Zionist invasion carried those heavy keys with them and kept them as symbols of their return to Jerusalem. When the father dies, the key is then passed to the oldest son. The front door led to a small open yard surrounded by the living rooms, and on one of its sides was the water well. Windows overlooking the outside alley were rarely found. Trees or potted plants were sometimes grown inside the yard, which was used for various family activities and as a playground for children. Sometimes in the summer, the yard was also used for sleeping.

A kitchen, as well as sanitary facilities, was accessible to the whole family. No special bathrooms were available. Bathing took place in a corner of the kitchen or the sleeping room.

Drinking water was taken from the well and kept in an earthen jar with a wooden cover and a metal can on top for drinking. Water, which was collected rainwater, was drawn from the well by a leather bail tied to a strong rope. If the water from the well was finished, residents had to buy water from a water vendor, called *saqqa'*, who carried fresh spring water on his back in large skin containers.

Walls of most Old City houses were over three feet (one meter) thick, which was necessary to support the heavy dome. Wide walls also provided protection against cold weather in the winter and hot weather in the summer. With such a thickness, windows could be used to sit in as well as for other uses. If windows overlooked the street, they were covered with protective iron bars for security and with a wooden blind, called *mashrabiyya* in Arabic, for privacy against prying eyes of passers-by. In the wide wall it was possible to have built-in closets where beds and bed covers were piled during the day and pulled out to be used for sleeping at night.

Some houses were composed of two stories, in the same style as described above, with the entrance to the upper floor from the inner yard. During the day, family members carried out their various house affairs, like cooking, sewing, and washing, in the inner yard. Children would play whatever games were popular at the time in the inner yard too. Sometimes, children were allowed to play outside the house, in the *hawsh*.

Some houses had rooms underground for storage of various household items or as stables for animals. Some of these stables extended beyond the underground boundaries of the house. In his memoirs, Wassef Jawhariyya describes how his father, at the beginning of the 20th century, had a white donkey and two stables, one outside the house with a door leading to the main road, and one inside in the underground floor, where charcoal and burning wood were stored, and that he and his brothers used to take care of the donkey on a daily basis.[2] He adds that three generations of the family lived together in the same house. When one of the young men of the family got married, one of the rooms was assigned to him. If a room was not available, an additional room was built, a small room was enlarged, or a large room was divided into two. This was done to keep the family members living together in the same house.

Most houses had modest furniture. The furniture in the sitting room was composed of mattresses covered by white sheets with hard pillows at the wall side to support the backs of sitting people, as well as in the middle of the mattress for people to lean on. Sometimes small tables were placed around the room. Depending on the financial state of the house owners, the floor was covered with carpets, rugs, or sheepskin. Sofas and chairs were introduced later.

The sleeping rooms were furnished with mattresses and covers that were placed on the floor over straw rugs at night and put away and stacked in the wall closet during the day. Iron and wooden cots were later introduced.

The person with the most authority at home was the grandmother (sometimes the grandfather). Everyone respected her and followed her instructions regarding division of work at home among her daughters and daughters-in-law. Mothers trained their daughters in cooking, embroidery, needlework, and all the necessary household duties expected of women. This was necessary for the girls to learn in order to be good homemakers when they grew up and got married.

The relationship between mothers-in-law and daughters-in-law was a source of amusement that gave rise to many humorous sayings. One of these is, "Cautery with fire is less painful than a mother-in-law at home!" When the grandmother died, the elder brother's wife took over her role, which often caused many problems among the women of the household.

Traditionally, people respected the household elder, be it the grandfather, the husband, or the elder brother. When he entered the house, children stopped shouting and playing and sat beside their mothers. His wife or daughter-in-law welcomed him by kissing his hand, taking off his shoes, bringing him some water and soap and a towel to wash his hands and feet at the water well located at the house entrance. After that she would give him his house slippers to put on. He would then go to his room where all family members would kiss his hand and sit with him silently until he started the conversation with the elders only. Children were not allowed to speak unless the grandfather asked one of them to recite a few lines from the Holy Qur'an or poetry. After that, all members of the family would have their supper together. Everybody at home would wait for the elder to start eating by saying loudly, "*Bismillah al-rahman al-rahim* [In the name of God, the merciful, the compassionate]." When he finished he would say, "*Al-hamdu l'Illahi Rabbi 'l-'alamin* [Thank God, Lord of the whole world]." Food was usually prepared by the daughters and daughters-in-law under the grandmother's supervision. Until the beginning of the 20th century, food was served at tables with short legs and eaten from one plate by the whole family, using hands or wooden spoons. Eating habits, however, changed with time. Until 1948, food was centrally prepared for the entire family and distributed among the various adjacent dwellings. After the 1948 war, sub-families started to move out to independent houses.

Having family meals together was a good chance for the children to acquire traditional habits that were considered good manners. Although the old habits were given supernatural explanations, most of them could now be rationally justified or scientifically proven right. The grandfather, for example, would insist that children wash their hands before and after meals, mention the name of God before taking food, eat with the right hand, as eating with the left hand was considered devilish, eat while sitting (the child was warned that Satan would snatch the food if one ate standing), not chatter while eating, and finish all the food on their plates, for all food thrown away would follow one on Doomsday. It was considered a bad habit to throw food on the ground, for food is God's gift that must be given due respect. It was a common habit among people when they saw a piece of bread on the floor to pick it up, kiss it, and put it on a high place for the birds to pick. This is said to be an ancient habit from the time of the Canaanites who considered wheat sacred. When people finished eating, they thanked God for what He had granted them. Children of the past believed in the strange reasoning for these instructions. Eventually, though, they became habituated to good manners no matter how they had been explained. When I tried to instill in my children these habits on the basis of the old beliefs, they laughed; at their school they had been given a more rational reasoning. Other than those related to food, there were, of course, many other good habits instilled into the minds of children using superstitious reasoning. One example was the necessity of washing hands seven times after playing with cats or dogs. In this case, the purpose was to make cleanliness a priority. Washing seven times originated from the ancient idea of seven as a sacred number.

There were social habits that brought people intimately together. Praying together at home or at the mosque or the church was one example. Visiting relatives, especially women who were married to men of other families, was another. On certain occasions, like feasts, men would pay visits to their female relatives, carrying a small gift with them. As children accompanied their fathers on these visits, the habit was instilled in them so that they would keep it when they grew old.

Children naturally acquire the habits of their elders. The following are some of the habits that were of great importance in traditional society in Jerusalem and the whole country.

Observing prayers was strictly adhered to. Children, whether Muslim or Christian, acquired this habit by seeing the importance given to it by their parents. In addition to saying prayers, there were other modes of worship which older people inculcated in their children, such as reading the Qur'an or the Bible, observing fasting during the holy month of Ramadan, or the forty days of Christian Lent.

Visiting female relatives, called *silat al-rahm*, especially females married to men from other families, was highly respected. This was done particularly during religious occasions, the purpose of which was to make the female relative feel that her male relatives were around and ready to support her. As children observed their elders follow this good custom, they grew up believing firmly in the necessity of it. It is a pity that the pace of modern life has made such a good habit obsolete.

A very important habit that the young used to acquire from their elders was greeting people according to time and occasion, as well as giving respect to elders and taking care of the poor. In addition to greeting parents at home, it is an old habit among Arabs in general to greet whomever one encounters at the street.

One of the good habits that were instilled in children's minds was the habit of work. Mothers trained their daughters to do all the household tasks, like cooking and cleaning. In certain cases, a mother might depend on her eldest daughter to take care of the younger children. Boys, on the other hand, would help their fathers in their shops, or in their workplace, and in this way they learned their father's trade.

One of the other habits that was highly respected and followed in our society was expressing good wishes to other people on personal and public occasions. Sometimes the occasion would happen at any moment. When someone drank, for example, people around him would wish him good enjoyment, or they might say, "From Zamzam, God wills," and the answer to the latter was, "Together!" Zamzam is the famous water spring in Mecca, which Muslims love to visit and drink from. The same was wished to one who takes the ritual wash (*wudu'*) before prayers. In fact, one can find that for anything one does, people traditionally have a special good wish.

All such customs made people feel that they belonged to one large family. The style of building in the Old City also helped people to be close to each other. In the new city, with its detached houses and wider streets, such customs were not easily adhered to.

In the old days, social security was not offered by the government, but people had their own social consolidation. When the head of the family died, or was imprisoned or exiled for political reasons, which happened often during the British Mandate, people would secretly help the affected family. This practice was particularly marked during strikes, especially the Great Strike of 1936, and revived during the Israeli occupation after 1967. Political strikes, and particularly curfews, were good occasions for men to get together with their neighbors and discuss current political affairs. Women, who were not usually included in political discussions, tended to spend the occasion doing household duties that needed cooperation with women neighbors. Curfews did not prevent people from moving from one house to another, for houses of the Old City, as mentioned earlier, were attached together in such a way that one could cover a good distance moving from one roof to another. This was also of great help for the revolutionaries.

The worst that people faced under the British (and face now with the Israelis) was when soldiers forced their way into houses looking for weapons and revolutionaries. The soldiers would savagely turn the house upside down in a vengeful manner. After the soldiers left, all neighbors would come to help put right what the soldiers had ruined, especially bringing in food to replace what had been destroyed. It is even worse today when the Israeli authorities decide to demolish a house at very short notice or sometimes without any prior warning. In this case, the whole neighborhood would challenge the military bulldozers with their bodies. When power prevails over courage, people quickly try to take out whatever furniture they can carry before the house is destroyed. The afflicted family is then given temporary shelter at the house of one of the neighbors until a place is arranged for them or their house is rebuilt. More than 2,000 houses were pulled down by the Zionists from the beginning of the occupation in 1967 until the year 2001. On June 9, 1967, the Israeli occupation authorities, in violation of international law, demolished 135 houses, two mosques, and two schools in al-Maghariba (the Moroccan Quarter) in order to make a large open space in front of al-Buraq (the Wailing Wall). Later, the house of Kamal Nammari was demolished in 1968 at Bab as-Sahira Quarter. Irrespective of the fabricated security reasons, the major reason for pulling down houses has always been political. Violation of building regulations was often used as a pretext. This criminal action had resulted in more than 435 families being rendered homeless. A number of children and old people had been buried under the rubble. It is obvious, however, that forcing Palestinians to leave their country has always been the ultimate goal of Israeli occupation.

Unfortunately, as a result of the Zionist occupation of Jerusalem, many old habits are now vanishing. Life has become difficult and expensive and poverty is widespread. As a result, people are becoming materialistic and can hardly cope with the heavy taxes imposed by the occupation authorities. In a research study conducted in 1997, Dr. Amin al-Khatib noted the following new phenomena in Jerusalem: addiction to narcotics and juvenile delinquencies; begging, especially among children; students skipping school and a lack of schools in Jerusalem and its suburbs; decrease in the average age of laborers; increase in religious fanaticism; general depression among people; lack of personal and social security; and the increase of spies, collaborators, and agents working for the occupation authorities.

As a result, people are gradually losing their previously strong family bonds. Many families are now physically scattered and those who happened to have been outside the country in June of 1967 were not allowed to come back home. In February of 1995, the Social Security Establishment announced that 15,000 of those who carry the Jerusalem identity card lived outside the city, while 60,000 of the original people of Jerusalem are deprived of all their rights.

The people of Jerusalem today feel as if they are being forced to live in a ghetto where life is unbearable. The municipal tax levied from the Arab inhabitants of Jerusalem amounts to 26 percent, whereas they receive not more than 5 percent of the municipal services.

Resolving Problems

Palestinian society, especially in the villages and small towns, used to seek judgment according to old Arab norms and traditions. This, in comparison with the official courts of justice, was a more effective way of having justice prevail. The whole family would take care of straightening out the behavior of its delinquent member(s). When the problem was grave, like a crime being committed, the protocol became quite complicated, and prominent men of other families or tribes were requested to interfere. After the British occupation of Palestine, those habits were more or less abandoned, especially in the cities. However, after Jerusalem and the West Bank were annexed to Jordan, this phenomenon re-appeared, as it was still being followed in East Jordan. And after the Zionist occupation, this habit was again renewed, for people wanted to avoid going to the Zionist courts.

2.
The Advent of Life

CHILDREN HAVE A SPECIAL STATUS in Palestinian society, for they are the legal heirs of the family and represent a normal defense against extinction, not only for the family, but also for the whole nation.

Due to the fact that the Palestinian society has been mostly agricultural, it has a characteristic culture regarding children. Parents who own land would like to see their children inherit it after they die. Children were expected to help their father cultivate the land when they were young, and to take care of their parents when they grew old. In Palestinian society, children kept the family together and strengthened their mother's status. A sterile woman was looked at suspiciously by society which might encourage the man to seek another marriage. Although sterility might have been from the husband's side, admitting sterility was disgraceful to him, therefore, it was the wife who was first to be blamed. If he was proven to be sterile either by his failure to have children from another wife, or by his wife having children from another marriage, then the blame would be ascribed to the effect of some wicked magic. In this context, there are many popular sayings that express the need for children: "She's ascending the mountain seeking a drug for pregnancy!" and "She's pregnant, feeds a baby, and four others follow her!"

In the past, societies considered it natural to prefer male over female children. For in traditional society, it was the male child who would defend his family and his country. It was also the male who would work and gain an income for the family, either by helping his father till the land in the countryside, working in town, or taking a job with the government, giving his family pride if the job was of high status. This made people compete to produce male children.

Girls, on the other hand, were considered to be dependent on the family, irrespective of the fact that, in the countryside, women worked like men, if not harder. On the grounds that they would eventually get married, girls were often denied their legal inheritance. This practice was justified by the fear that the family fortune would go to strangers. Nowadays, however, such habits have changed and women's status has tangibly risen. This change occurred when girls were given an equal chance for education, which resulted in a better work status for women. Some women have become college professors, bank managers, and even ministers, and others hold highly respected positions as physicians, engineers, and lawyers. In addition, events and social developments have proven that the connection of the girl to her family is stronger than that of the boy, even if she were married to a man from outside the clan. Furthermore, when a girl is well-educated, she can marry a man of her status, which reflects on the status of the girl's family.

Many people, irrespective of their social and educational standard, hoped for pregnancy immediately after marriage and would anticipate the good news of a missed menstrual period. Everyone observed the bride's behavior to see if it revealed the usual symptoms of pregnancy, like continuous nausea and an inclination to sleep, in addition to developing a craving for an odd kind of food. If she craved a food that was out of season, she would be given a mixture of olive oil, sesame, and butter cooked with onion and garlic. However, the bride would sometimes claim to have a craving for rare foods to test her groom's love. In any case, she was given special treatment regarding rest and food. In fact, people used to think that if the pregnant woman was not given the food she demanded, or if she looked at ugly things or animals, the child might be born with a birthmark, called *wahma* in Arabic. A newly pregnant woman was also not allowed to see ugly children; instead she was shown pretty children so that she would then give birth to a pretty child. Needless to say, this belief has no scientific basis, but still many people held it. If the symptoms of pregnancy did not appear, the bride, together with everybody at home, would be worried. The laboratory pregnancy test was not available at the beginning of the 20th century and the only reference for explanation was the midwife. It was shameful for women to go to a male doctor for a checkup. When pregnancy was confirmed, the good news was told to everybody, especially the bride's mother. The pregnant bride would then be the center of care from all members of the family.

If the bride's pregnancy was delayed, all kinds of superstitious explanations were put forward, the most common of which was the belief that a magic spell had been cast on her by some wicked woman who must be a relative of the groom. In this case, it was not a physician but a midwife that would help her. Sometimes, the midwife would give her a vaginal suppository that contained unknown contents. Treating a woman's infertility would also include some superstitious songs and dances. Many times the actual cause of delayed pregnancy was the fact that the bride was still biologically immature; for girls were sometimes married at the age of 10 or 11. As a doctor, I have encountered many such cases. Pregnancy was supposed to occur almost every year, otherwise the wife would be considered infertile. These beliefs and habits have changed a great deal.

The way women speculated on the gender of the embryo is interesting. Every woman gave her opinion and insisted on her experience in guessing whether the expected baby would be male or female. Some of the criteria used by women were the date the pregnancy occurred and its position in the zodiacal constellations, the shape of the mother's belly, the shape of her face, and the way she walked. When the baby was born, the women who guessed correctly would feel confidently proud, while those who made a wrong guess would resort to other explanations, or deny their guess altogether.

Very few mother-and-baby care centers were available in Jerusalem before 1948. In the Old City there was only one such center; it was sponsored by the American Colony and supervised by one nurse named Vera, who got to know most of the women and children in Jerusalem.

When the bride was confirmed pregnant, her mother and mother-in-law started preparing the baby's clothes. Around the end of the pregnancy, which was the most important time, the midwife would come to see the expectant mother and check the house. Only in difficult cases was a physician called or the mother dispatched to the hospital. At the beginning of the century, there were a number of midwives and only one governmental maternity hospital in Jerusalem located in al-Mascobiyya (the Russian Quarter). In her memoirs,[3] Rabiha Dajani mentions that an Arab Jewish midwife, called Khaya, helped her mother when she was born.[4] Due to limited transportation and the scarcity of telephones, families would usually deal with midwives living at a reasonable distance. Popular midwives were described as having "green" hands, denoting that they help bring more boys than girls into the world. People preferred old midwives who had finished their menstrual periods to avoid the possibility of a midwife having her period at the time of birth, because this was believed to be harmful to the mother and her baby. When the expectant mother was in her last months of pregnancy, especially if it was her first, her mother would visit her more often and, during the critical period in the final days, she would not leave her daughter until she gave birth. At such a time the whole neighborhood would be ready to help and the husband would not leave the house except to call the midwife. When signs of labor were noticed, the husband, accompanied by one of his relatives or neighbors, would hurriedly go to call her. The greatest problem occurred when the midwife was not found at home, in which case a search for her was nervously started. But the quasi-disaster came with the news that the midwife has gone to help another expectant mother whom she would not leave until she had delivered her baby. Another midwife would then be sought. But this one, as an indirect way of claiming a higher fee, would show discontent for being kept as a reserve, claiming that she was going to see another customer. Sometimes, when the midwife was late in coming, women of the neighborhood would have to help the mother-to-be deliver her baby. If the family was Muslim, during difficult births, women would read something from the Qur'an or put a necklace on the mother's stomach with the names of some saints or holy men. Men, children, and menstruating women were not allowed in. Only in the case of an extraordinarily difficult delivery, would the people around think of either calling a doctor or sending the woman to the hospital. Later, all pregnant women started going to mother-and-baby care centers or to maternity hospitals to give birth.

The moment the baby's head came down, everybody would be tense waiting for the rest of its body to reveal whether it was a boy or a girl. In case it was a boy, smiles would show on faces and one of the women would hurriedly go out of the room to pass the good news to the people waiting outside, especially to the husband, who was expected to pay the woman a *bishara*, which was a small amount of money or a gift of cloth. If the baby was female, especially if it was the first baby, smiles would disappear from the eager faces of the people around, who would try to pass the not-so-happy news to the mother with encouraging expressions such as, "Girls are better for their mothers than boys" or "You're still young, and tomorrow you'll fill the house with boys!" Whatever the sex of the baby was, after the delivery was done the midwife performed her technical duties of tying the umbilical cord with a thread of silk or a piece of cloth, then cutting it off and sprinkling some powder on the cut. Often, the thread, the powder, and the scissors were not sterile and the baby sometimes contracted tetanus. While the midwife tended to the mother, women inside the delivery room would thank God for the fact that the delivery was easy and the mother was in good health.

It was thought that a baby who was born with his hands open would be generous, otherwise he would be stingy. If its hands were open and placed around his head, he was said to be requesting God's help for his parents.

A'tiyyet al-Jora (The Ditch Gift)

Sometimes, the placental cord of a female baby was cut in the name of a male child, from among her relatives in the village, indicating that this newly born girl was promised to be the future wife of that boy. It is important to note that this was an irrevocable contract, unless later the promised bridegroom wished to revoke it.

After the placenta was removed, the midwife took care to put it in a container, keeping it away from the mother's eyes, until it was taken to be buried in a far away place where animals could not eat it. Otherwise, it was believed, the baby's health would be badly affected. For the same reason it was never thrown in the sewage ditch. The baby was then washed and its body covered with salt, for people believed that salt would strengthen the baby and protect it from fatal diseases. One of three possible procedures followed: the baby's body would be immersed in a salt-and-water solution, rubbed with salt and olive oil, or salt was added to the baby's body cover before it was wrapped with it. This was repeated from the baby's 7th day until its 40th. In Jerusalem, at the beginning of the 20th century, the newborn baby was not washed until it was seven days old. In some other towns and villages, babies were washed every day in the first 40 days. In addition to bathing the baby, the habit was to apply kohl around its eyes, for kohl was believed to be healthy for the eyes and protective against envy.

After the newborn baby was washed and dressed, peace prevailed after it was finally placed in the cot made ready for it. When the baby cried, women started thinking of such questions as whether its mother must feed it or not or whether her milk was available or not. On the grounds that Jesus Christ's food was mainly dates, which was why he was so fond of his mother, infants were given drops of water containing a paste of dates that were imported from Holy Mecca. Some pomegranate juice was also given to the baby, as people used to think that this fruit contained heavenly seeds.

For forty days, the mother would not be allowed to leave her bed, especially if it was her first child and particularly if it was a boy. Special food, rich in meat, vegetables, and fruit, was given to her and, with the purpose of enriching her milk, she was supposed to eat more than her usual quantity of food. During this period of time no woman having her menstrual period, in accordance with old beliefs, nor one who had recently had a baby, would be allowed to visit her. In case the mother's milk was not plentiful enough, the baby was temporarily given water sweetened with sugar and some herbs. If the mother did not eventually produce enough milk, the baby would be given to a close nursing relative or friend to provide him or her with her milk. This, however, had to be well thought out, and the woman who might feed the baby had to get permission from her husband. This was because, in Islam, boys and girls who take their milk from the same woman are considered brothers and sisters and are not allowed to be married to each other later on.

Since people believed that babies could die because of envy, especially from people with blue eyes, a blue bead and a piece of alum were conspicuously pinned to the baby's chest to neutralize any envious eyes which might look at it. Sometimes, an amulet, usually with a tiny copy of the Qur'an for Muslims, or a small cross for Christians, was fixed to the baby's head to protect him/her from adversities. Such an amulet is supposed to be kept throughout life. Such beliefs, which have faded away with time, originated from early history when people believed in the power of magic, imagining death or illness as a living creature that struggles with humans. I, personally, had an amulet that I did not believe in, but out of respect for my mother's wish, I continued to keep it around my neck until my last years of elementary school.

Granting names to babies depended on many factors. According to the old habits, the first boy of the family would be given his grandfather's first name and the first girl would be given her grandmother's first name. Otherwise, names were often chosen after the names of the prophets and saints, or after important historical figures, or because of certain occasions. Muslims, in general, were encouraged to name their boys after the Prophet Muhammad, or its derivatives, like Mahmoud and Ahmad, or to give them a name indicating submission to God, like 'Abdallah, which means worshipper of God. Such religious names, like 'Abdallah, Awadallah, and Nasrallah, are common among both Muslims and Christians. Sometimes, baby boys were given names of powerful beasts, like Asad (lion), Nimr (tiger), or Saqr (falcon), with the hope that they would acquire their strength. Girls were given sweet names like Zahra (flower), Abir (good scent), or Shaden (young deer). Nowadays, as the world is becoming smaller, people tend to use easily pronounced names. A phenomenon worth mentioning is that some Palestinians, after the disaster of 1948, tended to give their female babies the names of Palestinian towns and villages, like Palestine, Bisan, and Haifa. For boys, old, but expressive names, like Jihad, Nidal, and Kifah (all three meaning struggle), 'Awdah (return), and Thaer (revolutionary), have become popular among Palestinians, with the purpose of emphasizing their political cause.

Boys were always preferred for reasons that were particularly important in the past. A boy's birth, even if it was not the first boy, was much more celebrated than the birth of a girl. When the newborn baby was a boy, sweets were sent to relatives, friends, and neighbors, whereas if it were a girl, sweets would be offered to visitors only. Sometimes a mother whose offspring were all girls was looked at with pity. However, people usually made encouraging comments to a woman who gave birth to a baby girl. Nowadays, although boys are still preferred, girls are much more welcome.

At the birth of a baby, relatives and friends came to express their good wishes and offer gifts, like sugar and coffee, which were needed for the family's guests. With time, gifts changed according to modern life. A small piece of gold in the shape of the Holy Qur'an or the cross, for example, became popular. Guests were offered sweets, the most famous for the occasion is called *mughli*, which was prepared from semolina cooked with spices, sugar, and nuts.

The 40th day after delivery is very important for the mother. On this day, the mother, whether Muslim or Christian, took a bath to get rid of her *najasa* (impurity), in order to be able to observe her prayers and fasting. A Christian woman, with a newborn baby boy, was only allowed into the church after the lapse of 40 days after delivery, while if her baby were a girl, she would have to wait 60 days before being allowed into the church. After the 40th day, the mother could also perform her household duties and usually wore her best clothes and took special care with her makeup. She would also prepare special food for the 40th day occasion.

Today, after the uprising against the occupation in the West Bank and Gaza, one wonders what fate a Palestinian child encounters. In an impartial report by the Red Cross, published by *al-Ahali Magazine* on 5 May 2001, it was mentioned that before a Palestinian child is born, it has already learned the ABCs of siege, poverty, and sometimes death. When a baby is born alive, it may already be able to decipher the jargon of economics, occupation, and violence. All this is due to the harsh conditions of the security siege, the economic losses, and unemployment Palestinians face.

Grinding wheat, c. 1940's

3.
A New Family

MAN IS A SOCIAL CREATURE WHO NATURALLY tends to form a family and have children. Palestinian society had its own culture and customs regarding children and childhood. In Palestinian society, having children was considered the first and final objective of marriage. In addition, the marriage of sons, rather than daughters, was the essential source of happiness to the parents. Sons, not daughters, were considered the bearers of the family name, assuring its continuity and safeguarding its property and wealth. There were many motives that encouraged parents to ensure their son married early, such as the feeling that marriage would make sure he remained on the right path as regards behavior, and the fact that his wife would be a helping hand for her mother-in-law in the daily house-keeping duties.

Prior to the first thirty years of the 20th century, education was not widely available. Many people were barely able to read and write before they learned a handicraft so that they could begin working in order to earn a living, which would entitle a young man to get married. At that time, young men would get married between 18 and 20 years of age and girls between 13 and 15. When a young man was considered ready for marriage, his mother would start looking for a suitable girl among relatives and family friends. A suitable girl, besides being good looking, would be of the same social class as that of the boy, had good manners, and was well trained by her mother in cooking and home-management. When the family was not particularly well off, the girl was expected to be content with a simple life. When looking at a girl, the characters of her close female relatives were taken into consideration. Many old Arabic sayings show how a girl's living environment affected her manners. If a girl had been promised to a boy on the day of her birth, which would usually happen only among close relatives, she would not be allowed to marry anyone but him, unless he wished to release her from this bond. Otherwise, a girl's cousin usually had first priority over others to be married to her. There are many sayings in Arabic that describe this custom, like "A bride's cousin can make her dismount her horse [the horse she was riding on her way to her new home]." This means that if the bride was being married to someone else, and her cousin at the very last moment wanted to marry her, he would still be given priority. According to many sayings, marriages among relatives were strongly preferred. This was because of the idea that cousins were more likely to be understanding and compassionate toward each other than strangers would be toward each other. Still, there are other sayings that do not encourage marriages among relatives because of the schism it might cause in the family if the married couple did not get on well with each other.

Sometimes, perhaps to avoid paying a dowry, two young men would get married to each other's sisters. This, in Arabic, is called *badal* (exchange). However, this kind of marriage was not without problems.

Finding a girl for a young man had its rules. The girl's character was a most important factor in making a choice. Some girls (for instance, Bedouin girls) were described as being similar to an olive tree that needed hardly any care. A country girl was compared to a fig tree that required more care, whereas a city girl was compared to a vine tree that would demand a lot of care and luxury. The best homemaker was one who was a good home manager and who might encounter life with a lot of patience.

Due to the fact that men and women were unable to mix with each other, a young man would accept the girl chosen by his mother. The groom's mother, together with some of his close female relatives, would test the girl they had in mind before seriously considering her.

This was achieved by paying the girl's mother a friendly visit, the purpose of which was getting acquainted with the girl and her family in order to decide if they were fit for such an intimate relationship. Such a visit was made if the girl was not well known to the groom's mother. The tests performed in the old days may sound amusing to us: in order to find out if there were any abnormalities in the girl's physique, the boy's mother, or any of her close relatives, would hug the girl, passing her hand over the girl's body, and smell her breath. She would pass her fingers through the girl's hair to see if it was natural. Sometimes she would be given something hard, like almonds, to crack with her teeth and chew. They also tested the girl's speaking ability by asking her direct questions to see how she answered them. To test the girl's sight, one of the women would bring along with her a piece of cloth for embroidering. While she worked on it, she would unthread her needle and ask the girl to thread it again. If she did it successfully and quickly, then her sight was approved and she would be considered a good housekeeper. To test her way of walking, the girl was asked to fetch a glass of water from the kitchen. When she brought back the water, the visitors would watch to see if it was brought neatly or not, and also study the way she offered the water and what polite expressions she used.

When a girl was thought suitable by the family, the boy's mother would come with her request to the girl's mother, who would not give an answer before asking her husband. Some women made a living by arranging marriages, and often a matchmaker would take care of this proposal in place of the boy's mother. These women knew most young girls in town by virtue of their profession as peddlers or female hairdressers. Before giving his final acceptance, the girl's father would inform his extended family of the proposal, and would ask if any of the girl's cousins wished to marry his daughter. If none of her cousins wanted to marry her, the girl's family would start inquiring about the boy's family, manners, job, and financial position. If the man was known to have the habit of drinking alcohol or gambling, he would be immediately refused.

There are many sayings in Arabic that show what people

thought was a suitable marriage. These sayings encouraged a reasonable difference in age between the couple, discouraged the man from having more than one wife, discouraged the bride from getting married to a man who has children, and discouraged resorting to divorce in case of differences. The following are some of these sayings:

> A girl of good origin is better than one living in palaces;
> He who's married to a foreign girl will die of sickness;
> Take a man of craft, not a man of castle;
> He who has money can marry the king's daughter;
> He who wants a good and beautiful girl must be ready for her dowry.

As mentioned above, there are several sayings that discourage a woman from accepting a man who is married and has children. An example is: "Go to Akka and Arwad,[5] but don't take a man with *awlad* (children)." One that discourages men from getting married to two women is the following: "If you want to hasten your death, get married to two women!" The following saying shows how stepmothers are bad for the children: "A stepmother is God's wrath!" Something similar regarding a stepfather: "If you want his misfortune, let his stepfather take care of him!" Widows found remarrying difficult; but widowers found it difficult to remain unmarried. The following saying is quite expressive: "Unmarried for a lifetime is easier than being a widower for one month." When a divorced man or woman wanted to get married again, they would have to provide a convincing reason for their divorce, as people were always apprehensive about falling into the same problem.

In the past, it was the girl's father, without asking the opinion of his daughter, who made the final decision about accepting the man's marriage proposal or not. This habit is now obsolete.

Exaggerated though the stories of such conflict may be, it was common for there to be tension between the son's new wife and her mother-in-law, especially when they lived in the same house. Feelings of rivalry might also occur between the new wife and the wives of brothers. Again, there are many sayings on this matter, some of which are amusing. Following are a few examples:

> A mother-in-law will only love her daughter-in-law if the sea becomes a green paradise;
> I'd rather have my meals in Hell, than have my mother-in-law at home;
> A mother-in-law won't love her daughter-in-law even if she's one of Heaven's mermaids.

In the old days, early marriage was customary for many reasons. At the beginning of the 20th century, people used to think that marriage of teenage girls was likely to solve problems that might stem from the restricted life imposed on girls, and that they naturally needed a passionate relationship outside their family house. As sex outside marriage was (and in fact still is) taboo for girls, early marriage was thought to fulfill a girl's need for sex. In addition to this, girls used to believe that marriage would give them the chance to buy jewels and to have more luxury in life. As people strongly believed that a woman's job in life was to be a wife and a mother, they hastened to get their young girls married early. Early marriage for girls often had a negative effect on their children, for such marriage was likely to deprive young mothers of a sufficient education, which would be certain to help them better raise their children. Also, studies have shown that when a girl marries at a very young age, maturity may be delayed or not reached at all, even after a lapse of time.

Urbanization and the education of girls were two important factors in raising the marriage age. According to some statistics, however, an increase in early marriages was noticed during the beginning of the first intifada of 1987 in the 1967 occupied territories. The return of this phenomenon was ascribed to the long-term closing of schools by the Israeli army and the difficult economic situation caused by occupation. In addition, as the cost of marriage decreased due to the banning of wedding parties, it was a chance for young men to get married at low cost.

Education has also been a factor in changing the old marriage customs. As boys and girls mix with each other at college, they can now decide for themselves who they would like to marry. This has decreased the influence of their parents.

Although marriage among relatives was prevalent, during the

Ottoman era, at the beginning of the 20th century, young men intentionally sought marriage to women from other towns or villages for the purpose of being exempted from military service. This was to take advantage of a law that exempted men from military service if married to a woman who was fatherless, poor, and had no male relatives.

Among the Muslim population, acceptance of a young man's proposal was made known by telling the young man's family that the girl's father would be ready to see them at a specified time. This would prompt the elders of the groom to go to the girl's house and ask for her hand formally from her father. In the case of minor differences on matters like the amount of the dowry, a kind of delegation called *jaha* (men of nobility) would go to meet the elders of the girl's family with the purpose of reaching a compromise. Today, however, the *jaha* has become part of the proposal rituals and a kind of public announcement of the event. After the *jaha* is well received by the girl's family, the prospective bridegroom's father, or one of the family elders, gives a short speech thanking the girl's family for receiving them in accordance with the old and generous Arab traditions. In his speech, the speaker tells them that the purpose of their visit is to ask for the hand of their daughter, whose name is precisely pronounced, for their son, who is also precisely named. The speaker then expresses his hope that their request will be met according to the orthodox principles of God and His Messenger, the Prophet Muhammad. These speeches differ from one person to another, as some make a short speech and others make an elaborate one with quotations taken from the Holy Qur'an and old Arabic poetry. After this, the girl's father or one of her family elders makes a speech praising the suitor's clan and expressing their agreement to the proposal as a mark of honor to the noble men who formed the *jaha*. As a token of serious and mutual acceptance, everybody is asked to read the *Fatiha*, the first *sura* (chapter) of the Holy Qur'an. In addition to some sweets, Arabic coffee (without sugar) is then offered to the delegation, again as an indication that their request has been granted. After the recitation of the *Fatiha*, women in the adjacent room, in expression of their delight, utter the traditional *zagharid*, which are rhymed songs that have a related meaning. In the old days, after acceptance is given, the prospective bridegroom is allowed to enter the room and greet all the men there, starting with kissing the hands of his father, his father-in-law, and perhaps the elders of both families. Since the details of the dowry, the set of jewels to be offered to the bride, and the furniture of the house have already been agreed upon between the two families the *jaha* is only a formality and show of honor. In rare cases, perhaps when the girl's family decided to not carry on with the procedure, they would ask in front of the *jaha* for a dowry much higher than what had been agreed upon. In this case, which was considered bad behavior on the part of the girl's family, the man's family would either agree to any request or stand up to leave. Here the men in the *jaha* would interfere for a compromise. Traditionally, the dowry consisted of two parts, the first part was paid at the signing of the wedding contract, and the second was paid in case of divorce. The amount of the dowry depended on the financial position of both families. Nowadays, with the spread of education, quite a few families would ask for a dowry as small as one golden Ottoman lire as a first part. The second part ranges between 5,000 and 10,000 (Jordanian) dinars ($7,000–$14,000). The dowry was considered the property of the bride, in spite of the fact that in many cases her father took it for himself. In addition to the dowry, any presents that the bride received, as well as her personal income from her work, if she had any, and whatever she inherited from her family, were considered her personal property.

These days, the *jaha* has become a way to show off, especially when the bride's family demands to receive a large number of people including some of the notable men in the society. Sometimes, this large *jaha* is received at a five-star hotel that guarantees five-star bills!

In the old days, the couple might not have a chance to see each other before marriage. Later, they were allowed to go out together accompanied by a member of the family. Today, the couple may be allowed to go out together unaccompanied.

The Israeli occupation of Jerusalem in 1967 gave rise to radical changes in this very conservative society. Mixing between young men and women became commonplace, especially because of the tangible increase in living expenses that forced young women to work outside their homes. This did not increase the number of marriages, but raised its age. The fact that the occupation authorities had confiscated land and property was another important factor in decreasing the number of marriages; this was due to the decrease in available living units and the great rise in property rent. As young couples were forced to look for places to live outside Jerusalem, a large-scale migration took place, but those who left lost their Jerusalem identity cards and were unable to return. Thus, families were scattered and the family social structure and ties were weakened. Unfortunately, this has led to the appearance of negative phenomena among the people of Jerusalem, including theft and narcotics use. When I visited the Old City in 1998, I was pleased to see that people had resumed the old custom of having the newly married couple reside with the groom's family, so that they could avoid losing their Jerusalem identity cards if they left the city.[6]

Conditions for marriage among high-class families were quite strict. A young man wishing to marry a high-class young woman was accepted only if he also belonged to a high-class family, had a prominent post, and was well off. Having a good education would be an added asset. These families rarely accepted men of the lower classes or those originally from a village. Such restrictions, however, did not always benefit the girls, for they hindered them from getting married. After the 1948 war, when most Palestinians lost their property, which was illegally taken over by Israelis, unmarried women of high-class families, unable to take a post that might help them earn a living, became a burden on their families. One of the reasons for these restrictions was that rich families were afraid that their wealth would be inherited by strangers. Mixed marriages, however, became more and more acceptable in time.

At the beginning of the 20th century, for one reason or another and against the will of their families, some young Muslim men from the upper classes got married to Christian or Jewish women. Many of these marriages ended in divorce, but a few were successful.

Some of these women willingly converted to Islam. After the Israeli occupation of Jerusalem in 1967, the originally Jewish women were pressured to go back to Judaism, but they adamantly refused.

Marriage among Christians was not as complicated as it was among Muslims, because Christian young men and women, conservative though they also were, used to mix with each other and girls were not veiled. Still, the procedure followed by Muslims was the same for Christians. Scrutiny was even stronger among Christians, as most sects did not allow divorce.

After the engagement formalities, the wedding preparations began. For the low-income strata, such preparations were easy and inexpensive. The newly-married couple was given a room in the family house, or an extra room was built for this purpose. Furniture, which was usually mentioned in the wedding contract and was the bride's property, was simple and inexpensive too. Well-to-do families would start to look for a suitable house and prepare suitable furniture.

After the wedding date was fixed, the groom's family would begin inviting people to attend the wedding contract formalities. As invitation cards were not then in use, people were invited personally—men inviting men and women inviting women. Even when invitation cards became in vogue, some people would accept the card only from the hands of the groom's father or one of his brothers or close relatives. Sometimes, the person invited would refuse the invitation if the card was brought to him by a small boy or a stranger.

With a small and simple celebration, the marriage contract would take place at the house of the bride's father. Chairs were borrowed from the neighbors or, if necessary, from one of the cafés. When the *ma'dhun* (the sheikh authorized to underwrite the official marriage contract) arrived, he would sit between the father of the groom and the father of the bride, or their authorized representatives. In his register he recorded all necessary information about the marriage conditions. Then he would ask the two men to repeat after him a phrase to the effect that the bride's father agrees to have his named daughter be married to the named groom and the groom's father confirms his acceptance. In the past, many problems occured due to the fact that the *ma'dhun* did not see the bride prior to the marriage, and had no chance to find out if she was underage (which happened quite often) or if she actually accepted the marriage. As a practicing doctor, I saw quite a few cases where the bride was not more than 10 or 11 years old. In such a case, the father falsified the age of his daughter and, against the girl's will, he claimed her acceptance. Things today have changed, for the *ma'dhun* demands to see the girl, verify her birth certificate and identity card, and ask her personally if she accepts the suitor.

When the contract was signed, the guests would express their congratulations to the two families, take some lemonade and coffee, as well as a small purse filled with sweetened almonds, and the men would leave. Instead of the small purse, some rich families would give away boxes made of olive wood, sometimes ornamented with mother-of-pearl, filled with chocolates. A more expensive box would be made of silver. After the men left, the women remained to celebrate.

Soon after, preparations for the wedding began. The courtyard and rooms of the house were washed and sprayed with rose water, chairs were arranged around the place, and the major sofa of the wedding couple was placed at an elevated place in the courtyard, decorated with colored lamps. The wedding party was only for women.

Christians, on the other hand, almost always had the wedding contract at church. The groom's family took the bride from her parents' house with special words uttered as a kind of request that was given a polite answer. After sweets and drinks were offered, the bride would be taken to the church where the groom waited for her. Sometimes, the bride was handed over to her parents-in-law at the church.

Marriage Customs Among Some Arab Tribes

Some Arab tribes in East Jordan and Sinai have special marriage habits that are also followed in the villages around Jerusalem. The young man, after getting the girl's consent, would go to her father to request the girl's hand. The father then would ask his daughter's opinion, and negotiate with the prospective bridegroom on the dowry. There would be no religious formalities or celebrations. Once the dowry has been agreed upon, the bride would run away and the suitor would follow her. When he overtakes her, the couple would perform a token ritual. She would sit on a stone and he on another, then she would say to him:

> I sit on a stone, witness this, God of the people.
> I take you as my man, in the path of God and His Messenger.

The man would then respond:

> I sit on the soil, witness this, God of the world.
> I take you as my woman, in the path of God and His Messenger.

Then the married couple would break a straw, which is a symbol of unity. For when a straw is broken, it will never be back to its origin again. However, they were not considered united until the groom has performed his marital duty. Otherwise, the girl would be free to go back to her father's house.

Girl from Jerusalem wearing traditional Palestinian costume

4.
The Delightful Wedding Night (*huna*)

As marriage in Middle Eastern traditions is the most important stage in one's life after birth and circumcision (for Muslim male children), the wedding night is called "the delightful night." In Palestinian tradition, it is an occasion that every young man and woman dreams of and remembers throughout his or her life. Preparations for this night start right after reading the *Fatiha*, the first *sura* of the Holy Qur'an. This reading is a sign that the principle of getting married has been accepted by both parties.

The first thing the wedding couple and their families worry about these days is finding a dwelling place. In the past, it was a room in the family house, which, if not available, would be added on to the house and furnished according to the financial position of the family. In the villages near Jerusalem, the wedding dress was prepared bit by bit from the time of the girl's childhood. Every village has embroidery designs that are particular to it. Wealthy families prepared an expensive wedding dress for the bride that was a real piece of art. The bride was also very careful in choosing the various colors and models of her seven dresses. She and her mother kept these dresses a secret until the wedding night. These days, store-bought dresses are more readily available. The groom also carefully chooses his attire and has his outfit specially tailored.

The wedding party was also an important occasion for the relatives of the wedding couple to buy new clothes. These clothes, especially among women, were later remembered in connection with this event. Children also used to benefit from the wedding parties of their relatives and also got their share of new clothes and shoes. For in the past, unlike today, it was an accepted custom to take children to the wedding parties of their close relatives. This, of course, was a source of great pleasure for children. In villages, all residents of the village, old and young, attended wedding parties. In the city, where the party for women lasted until dawn, the women and children attending the party would sleep at the groom's house.

Wedding celebrations in Jerusalem, and most of Palestine, used to take an entire week and would culminate in the "delightful night"—when the groom and the bride spend the night together for the first time. The program, which differed slightly from one place to another, is described below.

The first night, called *al-hashwa*, was when the close female relatives of the groom went to the bride's house carrying with them perfume, henna, perfumed soap, and other cosmetics. The women of the bride's family would receive them with *zagharid*, the peculiar shrilling songs known all over the country.

The second night is called the "white night" because the bride wore only white clothes. On the third night, called the "henna night," all the women and most family members, old and young, applied henna to their hands in various decorations. In addition to its color, henna was believed to impart sexual vitality. Henna is made from the leaves of a specific tree—they look like olive leaves and have a good scent. There are two types, red and black. In addition to coloring hands, henna was also used for coloring hair, especially for masking white hair. In the old days, the same hairdresser who applied henna to the women would remove the bride's body hair. Removing body hair was done by a process called sugaring, which uses a thick cooked sugar as wax. The henna night was celebrated with singing and dancing, and women relatives and friends were invited to share the celebration. Throughout the day before the henna night, the hairdresser continued beautifying the bride and taught her how to walk in an attractive and graceful manner.

The fourth, fifth, and sixth nights were spent singing and dancing. On the evening of the seventh day, a delegation from the groom's close family members went to the bride's house to receive her. Very well dressed and beautified with perfect make-up, the bride was then ready to leave her family's house for her husband's. Today, almost the same customs are performed, except that many steps are modernized.

Kohl, or eyeliner, was an important beauty item. Arabs have been using it for thousands of years. It is taken from a special black stone that is called *ithmid* (antimony), which is crushed and turned into a fine powder that is kept in small ornamented silver jars. People used to think that, in addition to its value as a beautifying material for the eye, kohl had protective properties for the eye against ocular inflammations. It was also used as eyeliner for newborn babies on the grounds that, in addition to being good for the health of the baby's eyes, it was thought to be protective against envy. In fact, in the old Arab tradition, kohl was also used by men as eyeliner.

Two days before the "delightful night," the bride, together with a group of women from both families, marched in a parade, called *zaffa*, to a public bath that was reserved for the occasion. This arrangement was the duty of the hairdresser. The procession to the bath was either on foot, if the bath was in the neighborhood, or in chariots pulled by horses. After every woman had taken a bath, the hairdresser took care of the bride, massaging her, removing hair from her arms and legs, perfuming her body, and combing her hair. Between the afternoon prayers and sunset, the well-bathed and massaged bride went out to the sitting hall, followed by the accompanying women and professional singers hired to sing special songs for the occasion. These songs go like this:

> You, who prances like a branch
> You, brunette who has enchanted us
> May love's heart be burned
> For what it has done to us
> The daughter of the Arabs
> Insists on not dancing
> At the rhythms of the lute
> Unless she's relaxed
> And her candles are lit.

The professional singers of the old days were called *jinkiyyat*, plural of *jinkiyya*, after the name of an old musical instrument, the *jink*, which is similar to the harp. In addition to playing various musical instruments, the *jinkiyyat* also led the singing for weddings and similar occasions. Sometimes, the team included a blind male singer. Some historians believe that the *jinkiyyat* started the tradition of including a blind male singer after Napoleon's invasion of Egypt and the Syrian coast.

The wedding songs are thought to go back to the 9th century, when the Caliph Al-Mu'tamed married Qatr al-Nada, after whose name the popular song goes, "Oh henna, oh henna, Oh, Qatr al-Nada."

After the bath rituals, women took the bride back home, where she would sit on a raised podium surrounded by women singers and music players. All the women shared in the singing and dancing. The following day, the delegation from the groom's family came to take the bride to her new home. A special song that is known all over greater Syria and Iraq was sung on this occasion:

> She's leaving her father's house
> Going to the neighbors' house
> Wearing the white and the red
> With her eyes like those of a gazelle.
> I said to her, "Oh, I'm thirsty!"
> "Please show me your eyes!"
> And she said, "Go away, poor fellow!"
> "My eyes are those of a gazelle!"

As houses in the Old City were close to each other, the bride would walk in a *zaffa* (procession) to the groom's house, sometimes carrying a wooden sword. As the *zaffa* passes near a house, the women there utter their shrilling songs, *zagharid*, and sprinkle the *zaffa* with rose water or flowers and sometimes with rice. In certain cases, the bride is carried in a highly ornamented *howdaj* by four strong men. The *howdaj* is a small box that was used in the old days to carry women traveling on camel back. If the bride came from outside the Old City, she was carried in a *howdaj* on camel or horse back. As the bride's *zaffa* approached the groom's house, the women there welcomed her with a song like the following:

> A great welcome
> To our black-eyed bride
> What a tall palm
> Standing at the tall door

While the women in the *zaffa* sing the following:

> Open your doors
> Ornamented with flowers
> Let people say their good wishes
> And let everybody be happy

Words in these songs changed from time to time and from place to place, but the tune remained the same.

Once she arrived at the groom's house, the bride stepped into the house with her right foot first. Her mother-in-law would then give her a piece of dough in a vine leaf with a branch of peppermint and an olive leaf. The bride would take the dough and stick it with her right hand onto the wall near the door, indicating a blessed entrance to the house. If the dough fell on the floor, it was considered a bad omen for the house and family. According to certain customs, the dough was stuck to the door of the groom's room before the bride entered her sleeping place. Almost all of these customs have vanished with time.

The groom's *zaffa* to the public bath and back was almost the same as the bride's, except that it was for men only. In this procession, his friends would poke fun at him, sometimes pinching him, because it was thought to increase his excitement on his first night. Back when all the people of Jerusalem lived inside the Old City, the groom's *zaffa* would go out of the public bath toward al-Aqsa Mosque, where the *Maghreb* or *'Isha* (sunset or evening) prayers were duly attended before the parade went home. In that *zaffa*, the groom walks in the front line, surrounded by his brothers, cousins, and friends, with two dancers playing the sword and shield in front of the *zaffa*.

The classical songs sung during this *zaffa* have remained the same from the old days until today, sometimes with a bit of change in words. An example is

> We've come, we've come, and we've come
> We've brought the groom and come
> Our groom is the star of all the youth
> He's the star of all the youth
> Our groom is the son of Jerusalem
> He's the son of Jerusalem
> Our groom is Antar of Abs[7]
> Antar of Abs is our groom
> We're invited to a pleasurable wedding
> And it's our duty to go
> You pretty girl at the roof
> Look down and see our men

When the *zaffa* reached the house, women's singing and *zagharid* got higher. As the groom reached the wedding hall, which was full of women only, he entered backward, while songs were sung and *zagharid* were trilled loudly. An example is the following:

> When the full moon visited us
> Oh, my eyes
> The lights intensified
> Verily intensified
>
> Please call for the groom
> Let me see him
> Let me see his white neck
> With his couple of beautiful birthmarks
> Please call for his mother
> Let her tailor his suits

Then, accompanied by his father or one of his brothers, the groom went up to the raised podium where he sat to wait for the bride. Then the bride, accompanied by her mother or sister and the hairdresser, came in walking shyly and gracefully toward the podium. As she approached, the groom came down from the podium, pulled up her veil, and took her up to the podium where she sat beside him. In the old days, this was the first time he saw her face. At this moment, proper singing starts, and women show their art of dancing.

The songs sung at this moment were usually songs of welcome:

Blessed let it be
Seven times blessed
The way Muhammad was
On Mount Arafat blessed
Prayers be on Muhammad
Blessed is the day
And may every beloved one
Have the same.

O groom's mother
Let things be well done
Let seven female slaves serve you
While you sit in grandeur
But if you don't dance
I'll be cross with you

The wedding party was an occasion for great joy, but it was also an occasion for social solidarity. Close relatives and friends contributed money, called *nuqut,* to the married couple. The idea was to help the couple start their married life. This financial help was considered a kind of loan—the groom or his father was expected to pay it back on similar occasions, or it may have been already paid on similar occasions. This habit is still followed today despite the many changes that have taken place.

The bride would not sit on the podium the entire time. Every now and then, she went out to change into one of her seven dresses. Every dress was a different color, for a different song and a different dance. Usually the bride carried two candles in her hands or several small candles each stuck on one of her fingers, to enlighten her. This was an old habit that is rarely followed now. By dawn the wedding party was over. The bride would have changed into her seventh dress, which was usually made of black silk, and danced what is called "the coffee-man dance," carrying a coffee pot in one hand and a cup of coffee in the other, while singing a special song. At the end of the party, the chief *jinkiyya* (singer), together with the groom's mother and the bride's mother, led the couple to their bedroom. On the wall of the bedroom both the groom and the bride would stick a piece of dough kneaded with mint and olive leaf as a sign of good fortune and for fertility in the marriage. As the wedding couple entered the bedroom, the women outside continued singing while the couple did their marital duties. Sometimes, the two mothers waited at the bedroom door to receive the good news that the bride was a virgin. This was proved by showing a white cloth stained with blood, a sign followed by a loud *zaghruda* uttered by one of the women. This old habit has vanished.

The marriage bond was highly respected. Divorce, therefore, was rare. In fact, a wife used to believe that living with her husband and children, no matter how unhappy she might be, was better for her than living as a divorced woman at her father's house; worse would be living at her brother's house. Nowadays, as women work and earn their own income, and especially after the 1967 invasion and occupation, the divorce rate has shown a marked increase.

The same wedding procedure applied to Christians as well, except that the Christian bride's *zaffa* ended at the church where marriage formalities took place.

One week after the wedding celebration, the married couple, whether Muslim or Christian, visited the bride's family where they were received with singing and dancing and where they ate lunch and received gifts. After that, their close relatives invited them for meals. The Christian bride and groom would go to the church first to pray, and the bride wore a black dress for this occasion.[8]

Until the 1950s, taking a honeymoon was unknown to Palestinians of all social strata. After the 1950s, taking a honeymoon became a habit followed by most people. At the beginning, it was a matter of spending one night in a hotel outside of Jerusalem. As transportation became easy and affordable, wedding couples started spending their honeymoon abroad, particularly in Egypt, Syria, or Lebanon.

It is important to say that while Palestinians after the Israeli occupation became less joyful, they were also keen on celebrating wedding parties as a challenge to the occupation authorities. Songs were adapted to express this challenge, and now bear a tinge of melancholy. However, it remains a fact that the occupation has spoiled most of the habits and social bonds described above. In fact, because of the occupation, we have been deprived not only of our country, but of many of our traditions. This is a tragedy that remains untold.

Sword dance at a wedding

CHAPTER FOUR: THE DELIGHTFUL WEDDING NIGHT (HUNA)

The children of the Husseini family of Jerusalem in front of the St. George's Anglican School. (c. 1936)

5.
Our Children, Our Souls

CHILDREN, AS THE HOLY QUR'AN DESCRIBES THEM, are the ornaments of life. In the past, right after the first day of marriage, the wedding couple and their family looked forward to having children, and people around would wish them both prosperity and abundance of children. Children had their mother with them all the time, as women rarely worked outside the home. They were also breast-fed for almost two years, enjoying all the benefits of breastfeeding. Since extended families used to live together, children were constantly surrounded by their parents, grandparents, uncles, aunts, and cousins. Living with such a large family was usually psychologically healthy for the child, who would gradually imbibe from the elders around him some of the best old Arab traditions. On every occasion, such as bathing their children or combing their hair, mothers used to sing special songs; these songs handed down beneficial ideas that were an important factor in forming the child's personality. This lifestyle is dissimilar to our modern society, where mothers often go out to work, leaving their children with nannies or in day care.

Breastfeeding was highly commended in the old days and almost all mothers breast-fed. If for some reason a mother could not breastfeed, she might give her newborn baby to a relative or friend who was breast-feeding at the time, so that the baby could feed from her breast. Children who fed from the same mother were considered sisters and brothers and were not allowed to marry each other later in life. If an alternative lactating mother was not available, cow's or sheep's milk would be used. This milk was given to the baby immediately after being boiled and cooled down, as refrigerators were not available. The old generations believed that breastfeeding was ordered in the Holy Qur'an by this verse: "Mothers shall suckle their children for two whole years." It is also referred to in the following verse, "We enjoined man to show kindness to his parents, for with much pain his mother bears him and he is not weaned before he is two years of age." Some of the old sayings show that people believed that breastfeeding was healthy for children. When they wanted to describe a man as strong and healthy, they would say, "He's been fed with his mother's milk." When someone did a good deed, people would say, "Blessed be the breast that fed him!" Some of the old explanations for the good value of breastfeeding might have been unscientific, but the end result matches the modern scientific discoveries of the merits of breastfeeding. It has recently been proven that breastfeeding has healthy consequences for the baby and its mother as well, both psychologically and physically.

In order to get the baby to sleep after being fed, the mother sang to him while rocking him in a swinging cot. Poor families made this cot from a large piece of cloth or jute attached to two ropes with a piece of wood at the baby's feet and another at the head. Inside this primitive cot a tiny mattress was placed and the cot was hung from two high beams. Sometimes, a long rope was attached to the cot so that the mother could swing the cot from a distance when the baby cried and she wanted it to sleep again. It has recently been proven that swinging a small baby is bad for the brain; but this fact was unknown in the old days. Usually a piece of light cloth was put over the baby's cot to protect the baby from flying insects.

The baby's bath was great fun for mothers and family members. The baby was put in a small tub and washed. Gently and gradually, its body would to be immersed in warm water, and his mother—together sometimes with the whole family around—would sing the baby songs that had an amusing rhythm. The words in most of these songs had a simple meaning, but they were expressive of the old traditions. An example is:

I strip you of an unhealthy dress
I dress you with a healthy dress
I strip you of a dirty dress
I dress you with a clean dress
God is careful
May He grant us our clothes
I strip you of an amulet
I put on you two amulets
One of Al-Hasan
Another of Al-Hussein[9]
Day and night
The two shall guard you

In addition to the mother's care for her baby's cleanliness, she was also careful about combing his hair and dressing him with clean and pretty clothes. All this was also accompanied with special songs. An example is:

May God bless him/her
Bring him/her the bottles of scent
This small one, this small one
May I see him/her grow up

The family house in the old days was the place of mothers. Traditionally, women did not work outside the house, except as teachers at girls' schools, though most women did not get enough education to be qualified for that work. This had the merits I mentioned above, of establishing a close bond between mother and child, and allowing children to imbibe Arabic culture and habits. Of course, women should be given equal chances as men in both education and work, it was not so at the time.

Newborn infants were swaddled tightly for a few weeks, a practice that is almost abandoned nowadays. People believed that swaddling made the infant feel more secure, as it might mimic the feeling of being in the mother's womb. According to older generations, swaddling was thought to protect the infant from abdominal pangs and nausea, and from suffering sprains. However, babies sometimes suffered from a body rash while being swaddled, most likely due to being wetted by its urine and feces.

For superstitious reasons, older generations did not encourage kissing babies. This, however, is in line with modern medicine that has proven the bad effect of kissing a baby, especially mouth to mouth.

To a great extent, traditional baby songs, passed from one generation to another, are still being sung today. This has a positive effect on both baby and mother; the mother feels good as she sings to her baby and the baby becomes relaxed listening to its mother. In fact, various songs accompanied children throughout the different stages of their young lives, each expressing a certain activity.

The piercing of female baby's ears, which the midwife used to take care of, was done soon after birth. To do this, the tip of the needle being used would be burned on a candle flame. As the needle was pushed through the ear, a thread of silk attached to the other end of the needle was pulled through the new hole, and was then kept with a knot for a long period of time to maintain it. If the pierced place became inflamed, olive oil or other ointments were applied. Later the thread was removed and replaced by an earring. Today, a modern instrument is used for this purpose.

At the age of four and six months, baby boys and baby girls respectively were trained to sit, using pillows to support them until they could sit without help. Both were encouraged to crawl on the floor, until they could stand on two feet and walk. At this time, the whole family joyfully shared in helping the child walk. The date when the baby walked for the first time was remembered. The earlier it happened, the more pleasure it gave to the family, because it was considered a sign of good health.

Toys were very simple and mostly made at home. Children, due to being with their mothers and family all the time, were much happier than present day children are with their sophisticated toys. Nowadays, most mothers work outside the home and their children spend much less time with their family. Besides, unlike domestic help today, who often come from foreign countries and do not speak Arabic, domestic help in the past came from local society and were able to impart to children a lot of our culture. This inability to speak

Arabic on the part of domestic helpers today obviously hinders the child's ability to learn quickly. One must also not forget the other factors peculiar to Palestinians that have had a negative effect on children's learning ability, especially the negative economic and social situations that the Zionist occupation has caused.

The appearance of the first tooth was again a reason for celebration. The family offered a special sweet desert called *sinuniyya*, an Arabic word derived from *sinn*, meaning tooth, to the relatives, neighbors, and friends who came to congratulate. *Sinuniyya* is composed of cooked wheat, nuts, and raisins. Other cities and villages have other kinds of sweet desert that they offer on this occasion. When children lost their baby teeth later on, the old habit was that the child threw his/her old tooth in the face of the sun and shouted, "Oh sun, take the tooth of the donkey and give me the tooth of a deer."

Mothers used to breastfeed their infants for as long as possible, perhaps following the verse in the Holy Qur'an mentioned above that sets two years as the proper period for breastfeeding. However, some mothers resorted to breastfeeding their babies as a natural means of contraception, as many women would not conceive while they were breastfeeding their babies. This, however, did not always work, as some mothers would become pregnant as soon as forty days after giving birth. When the child was weaned, usually against its will, it was given rice pudding cooked with milk and vegetable soup, until it becomes used to adult food. If the child resisted being weaned, the mother, with the objective of making him/her dislike her breast, applied some bitter material to her nipples.

Weaning the first child meant preparing for another pregnancy. A mother in her second pregnancy received less care than in her first pregnancy, but the expectation of the next baby's sex was still highly anticipated, especially if the first baby was a girl. When a boy was born after a girl, a great celebration was made, and special songs were sung, like the following *zaghruda*:

> O people, make your blessings to the Prophet
> O people, the mother of girls has had a boy!

The celebration was even greater when a boy was born after a few girls. Still, when a girl was born after a few boys, the family welcomed her with the following *zaghruda*:

Girls are our wish
And our boys are so many
Thanks to you God
Our daughter-in-law has given birth

As the family grew, the father's responsibility became greater and the mother was expected to be careful about her expenditure at home. The clothes of elder children were usually given to the younger ones and the mother was expected to patch up and mend the torn clothes of her family in order to minimize expenses. This was accepted by society so long as the clothes were clean.

In the past, when children grew up and their mother was unable to control their mischievous behavior, she would try to please them by making simple toys for them or showing them how to make them. Sometimes she would smack them or tell their father to do so; or she might tell them about fabulous demons that would hurt them if they were naughty. With better education on the part of the parents, these habits are now almost gone. Children nowadays receive their tales from the television, which shows them all kinds of fabulous creatures that have become part of their daily life, so threatening them with fabulous demons when they are naughty no longer has the same effect.

As I mentioned earlier, there were three important stages in male childhood: birth, circumcision, and marriage. Today, getting an education has overshadowed all that.

Circumcision is an old habit that is followed by Muslims and Jews. It is believed to be of ancient Egyptian origin and the first man in recorded history to be circumcised was Abraham. In his wake, Jewish law dictated the necessity of circumcision. Strictly speaking, Abraham was not a Jew, but the three Abrahamic religions believe in him as the first prophet who worshipped God as the only creator. Circumcision was considered a means of purity that was imperative for males to have. According to the old beliefs, a man could not slay birds and animals for food if he was not circumcised. Circumcision was an occasion for celebration. In the past, it was a great celebration that perhaps expressed the respect given to males by society. Usually circumcision was done at home, but sometimes, if the parents had made a vow, it would be done at a sacred place, like al-Aqsa Mosque. Circumcisions were performed by some specialized barbers soon after birth, but the event might be postponed to forty days after birth. This minor operation was performed by removing the foreskin of the penis with a sharp knife. A well-trained barber did it quickly, and then waited for 2 or 3 minutes to see if there was any bleeding. He would then apply some antiseptic powder on the incision and wrap the penis with clean gauze. The next day or 2 days later, the "surgeon," so to speak, came back to see if the wound had healed and his job was completely done. Sometimes, heavy bleeding occurred when a vein was cut by accident. If the instruments were not well sterilized, the wound could become infected. In such cases, the baby had to be taken to the hospital. Fatal cases were not unusual. In the villages, due to the scarcity of specialists, circumcision was delayed until a few boys could be circumcised together in a massive celebration that was similar to a wedding. There, the person who performed the circumcision was taken on horseback into the village in a *zaffa* like a groom at his wedding. He dressed in white clothes, a white cloak, and a white, embroidered hat. Special songs were sung on this occasion.

As circumcision was also practiced by Jews, some Muslims at the beginning of the 20th century called on Jewish specialists to perform circumcisions. When awareness of the political intentions of Zionists exacerbated relations between Muslims and Jews, many Muslims no longer accepted Jews carrying out circumcisions.

Some specialized people still perform circumcision today, but the majority of circumcisions are done at hospitals by a qualified surgeon right after birth.

The Christian community celebrated the baptism of their children. This event usually took place before the child reached his first birthday. The preferred date for baptism was January 6th, the feast of Epiphany, which is the day the Magi visited. Otherwise, it would be done on any Sunday. The child's father chose a godfather and godmother from among his relatives, or sometimes he would choose an important man from the society as a way of seeking good relations with him. The godfather usually distributed candles and paid the priest's fees. Baptism is celebrated by Christian Palestinians the same way circumcision is celebrated by Muslims. Special songs similar to those of circumcision are sung on this occasion. In the old days, female children were baptized without celebration.

Diseases were common among children, especially at the beginning of the 20th century and before. This was due to the fact that vaccinations were still unknown and people were unaware of health care, in addition to the absence of doctors and birthing centers. People used to attribute diseases to bad demons and to envy. That was why they would attach a piece of alum and a blue bead, or a small copy of the Holy Qur'an, or a small cross to the child's clothes. When a child fell ill, his grandmother would read him some Qur'anic verses and burn incense in the house with some table salt. When the salt crystals cracked as they burned, it was thought that the envying eye was also cracking. Sometimes, one of the "men of God" was called upon to carry out this ritual. Children with abdominal pain used to be given carminatives from brewed local herbs. Sometimes the abdomen was massaged with lukewarm olive oil. There was an old habit of massaging the baby's body with olive oil from the time of its birth. Although these habits are now being abandoned to modernity, some scholars still believe in the psychosomatic benefits of this massaging on the grounds that the skin, at this stage of a child's life, is one of its most important body organs for contact with the outside world. As the skin develops, the child's nervous system develops in a more balanced way that could lead to better disease resistance.

There were several other methods for treating sick children. For diarrhea, milk was replaced with yogurt, with an infusion of bitter plants, such as pomegranate peel. For umbilical hernia, a piece of metal, wrapped with cloth, was put directly on the navel, wrapped up well there, and left for some time. For a skin rash on the upper thighs, olive oil with salt was applied, sometimes mixed with red earth. There were, of course, many other diseases and remedies, but the list is too long to mention here. However, the psychological disorders caused to children by the Israeli occupation are still without remedy.

School children (early 1940's)

6.
Learning is Enlightening

FROM THE DAWN OF OUR MODERN HISTORY, Jerusalem has been the city of scholars and schools that were connected either to the al-Aqsa Mosque or to the various churches in town. The religious status of Jerusalem worldwide gave rise to a number of literary, cultural, and political societies and clubs, especially at the turn of the 19th century. Learning was quite prevalent among the higher and middle classes of the society, and to a lesser extent among the lower classes.

Learning the Holy Qur'an by heart during childhood was customary for Muslims in the city. Children accompanied their fathers to prayers at al-Aqsa and other mosques, where they would listen to the readers reciting verses of the Qur'an. They were also sent to private coaching, similar to kindergartens, called *kuttab*, where, in addition to the learning the Qur'an, they would be taught elementary reading, writing, and arithmetic. Children going to *kuttab* carried their copy of the Qur'an and their slate in a bag made of cloth with a long strap that went over their shoulder. The slate was used for writing with chalk, as paper notebooks and pencils were unavailable. At the beginning of the 20th century, trousers were not acceptable as male dress; instead, children wore the traditional Arab male dress, called *jilbab*. The *kuttab* room was spacious, and its floor was covered with a rug of straw, called *hasira*. The teacher, called the sheikh, would sit at the end of the room on a slightly raised mattress, holding a long stick in his hand with which he could reach all the pupils sitting in front of him. The younger pupils sat in front and the older students lined up behind them. Reciting and learning the

Qur'an by heart was the most important lesson. The sheikh would read the Qur'anic verses loudly and the pupils would repeat them a few times after him. Then the pupils would recite the verses together a few times before each pupil was asked to recite them alone. When the pupil read correctly, the sheikh uttered an encouraging word to him, otherwise, he would be reprimanded for the first mistake, and smacked with the long stick for repeating his mistake.

At the *kuttab*, the pupils were also instructed on good manners and cleanliness, and were told tales that supported what they were taught. At the beginning of the 20th century, there were many *kuttabs* in Jerusalem, but the number diminished as more modern schools were established.

There were also a few foreign kindergartens that gradually increased in number because more children wished to start school at an early age. Government schools used to accept children into the first elementary class at the age of seven, but private schools were more lenient. After the 1967 Israeli occupation, kindergartens increased in number, due to the establishment of many charitable societies by volunteers offering help to people as a kind of peaceful resistance to the occupation. Many of these societies had their own kindergartens.

When a student completed reading the entire Holy Qur'an and memorized part of it, it was an occasion for a great celebration. During the year this happened, preparation started early by buying new clothes, usually a white Arab dress called *qumbaz*, a white headdress called *hatta* or *kufiyya*, tied with white rope, called '*iqal*, and a pair of shoes, again preferably white. The celebrating pupils marched together in the quarter or the village, carrying white or colored flags, together with the Palestinian flag, and singing various religious anthems. Depending on their financial position, families also celebrated the occasion on their own and received congratulating relatives and friends.

Schools in Jerusalem were of various kinds and curricula. Public schools during the British Mandate were relatively weak. Private schools were either national or connected to Western religious missionaries. The curricula in the former emphasized Arab and Islamic culture and history, especially as indigenous society was facing a British Mandate that was facilitating the Zionist endeavor to move Eastern European Jews into Palestine. In the morning parade, just before classes began, all pupils would sing the various national anthems with their beautiful words. The anthems were written by well-known Arab poets, both contemporary and old, with words that charged the pupils with Arab national pride. Many of the graduates of those schools became active members of the national resistance against the British Mandate and Jewish immigration to Palestine. Missionary schools, on the other hand, were connected to various European countries, emphasizing European culture and history and teaching in different European languages: English, French, German, or Italian. All pupils at those schools, even non-Christian, had to study material taken from the Old and the New Testament and to attend church services.

One thing must be noted about teachers in Jerusalem, as well as in most Palestinian towns: they were highly dedicated to their profession that was looked on as a noble mission, not a job for earning money. Teachers, therefore, were much respected by the society and considered part of its elite. The great 20th century Arab poet, Ahmad Shawqi, wrote a famous poem in praise of teachers, the first line of which goes like this:

> Stand up and give due respect to the teacher
> For the teacher is almost a prophet.

In fact, the teacher used to give his pupils not only knowledge, but good manners and patriotism too. In comparison with many teachers today who give private lessons after school as a way to increase their income, those in the past, motivated by their sense of dedication, gave extra lessons to their weaker pupils free of charge. They considered their pupils a national project requiring all possible help to achieve success. In turn, pupils did not let their teachers down, for many of the national schools were practically citadels of patriotism and good suppliers of men and women for the national movement. As a result, there was rarely any perversion on the part of the pupils.

This wholesome relationship between teachers and their pupils resulted in productive cultural, artistic, and sporting activities. Reciting Arabic poetry by heart was one of the most popular cultural activities at schools. Pupils were also encouraged to read books and discuss them together. A few literary and artistic societies and clubs appeared after World War I in Palestine, as an expression of the political and cultural activity that took place in the country between 1918 and 1920 after the British occupation of South Syria (Palestine and Trans-Jordan). Such societies had both Muslim and Christian members, and used the symbol of a cross inside a crescent to stress Muslim and Christian unity against the British and the Zionists. The Arab Club, established in 1918, was the most famous club in Jerusalem. A few of the Palestinian national figures were members of the Arab Club, and its major objective was defending the nation's independence. In line with this, the Arab Club sponsored many political and cultural activities aimed at defying the British Mandate and the Zionist immigration.

National schools often staged plays with patriotic themes taken from victories in Arab history. Examples of these plays were *Liberation of Jerusalem*, *Saladin*, and *Khaled ibn al-Walid*. Missionary schools, on the other hand, staged foreign plays like those of Shakespeare.

Sculpture and painting were quite rare, but tangibly increased after 1948 and particularly after 1967. Musical orchestras were also formed, the most important of which was the Islamic Orphan Institution Orchestra.

After the Israeli occupation, due to being controlled by the Israeli Ministry of Education and the Municipality of West Jerusalem, most schools in East Jerusalem faced a decline in the standard of education. The occupation authorities tried to change the curricula in East Jerusalem with the objective of brainwashing the pupils to accept the Israeli narrative. Compounding this trouble, private national schools became unable to recruit competent teachers. This, along with security measures being enforced against Palestinians, brought the standard of education down.

Control of children by their families also weakened as a result of the generally troubled atmosphere created by the occupation. This atmosphere had a bad effect on the public's former interest in literature, poetry, and theater. A small segment of society was naturally exempt from this statement. The result, as to be expected, was a prevalence of substandard songs and bad behavior among the younger generation, combined with a strained relationship between teachers and pupils. Still, this situation did not have a negative effect on the pupils' patriotic attitude towards their homeland in its struggle against the occupation forces. In fact, the first intifada in 1987 broke out because of activities of the younger generation, mostly school pupils and university students, both female and male. Many young people were killed or imprisoned by the occupation army, including a large number below the age of fifteen.

A scout movement started in Jerusalem early on after the occupation in 1948. A number of scout corps formed in various schools. This had the positive effect of instilling in pupils a love for their country and sincerity for their people's cause. Scouts had their own beautiful anthems for patriotic occasions that filled them, together with their audience, with great zeal. One of those anthems had the following words:

> Oh Palestine, may God protect you,
> My soul and blood are sacrificed for you.
> You're not a piece of land, you're a piece of heaven
> You're the birthplace of Jesus and
> The homeland of the magnificent al-Aqsa.

The Scout's oath goes like this, "I pledge by my honor to do my best, to do my duty towards God and my nation, to help other people at all times and to obey the scouts' law."

Whether in Jerusalem or in the whole of Palestine, sports activities were popular during the British Mandate, especially at private national schools. Gymnastics and football (soccer) games were daily activities at schools, but the most important event was the annual sports festival, the preparation for which would take place a few months in advance. The annual sports festival at some national schools was a great patriotic day, attended by the top Palestinian leaders, with the scouts and musical bands marching through the streets of Jerusalem. Unlike national schools, missionary schools during the British Mandate used to have their annual festival under the auspices of the British High Commissioner. It was, therefore, unpopular. Such festivals came to an end after the Israeli occupation.

Football tournaments among schools used to attract a great number of spectators. When a tournament took place between a national school and a missionary school, only the team of the national school was hailed by the audience, irrespective of its performance. Tournaments sometimes resulted in fights among the audience cheering on the teams. Football fields in the 20th century were mostly primitive, lacking the modern facilities known today. The YMCA had the best and most famous football field, built in 1924.

Sports activities at girls' schools were smaller in scale and without an annual festival. Instead, girls were more active in domestic science. Teaching the domestic sciences used to start gradually in elementary classes; in secondary classes, pupils were theoretically and practically trained in cooking, embroidering, dressmaking, together with taking good care of one's house. Later, training in typewriting was also given, sometimes as part of the domestic science program.

Despite poverty, Palestinians in general have dedicated a lot of effort toward learning. On finishing secondary school, pupils had to sit for the Palestine Matriculation Exams that were arranged by the Department of Education during the British Mandate, then by the Ministry of Education after the union between Trans-Jordan and the West Bank. Pupils at foreign missionary schools had to sit for the London Matriculation Exam. I studied at al-Mutran (St. George) Secondary School, which was a missionary institute. We had a very bad relationship with the Jewish pupils, but there were no clashes with them, as the British headmaster was very strict, and sometimes very cruel, particularly with Arab pupils. Unfortunately, he treated Arab pupils in a very arrogant manner, paying no attention to our loud protests. He gave strict orders that all pupils must speak English only, with a fine of 5 piastres levied from those who did not abide by his orders. That was a large amount of money for pupils at the time.

The matriculation exam was an important stage in the pupil's life, for it was a necessary qualification for many posts in the government and at banks. A few of the graduates joined their family businesses, or if they belonged to a rich family, they attended a university in other Arab countries like Iraq, Egypt, and Lebanon. Foreign universities, especially Cambridge and Oxford, were highly respected, but only very rich people could afford them. Scholarships granted by the British government to pupils with high marks were only for literary, non-professional fields of specialization. In the past, women were less fortunate in getting the chance to go to university.

After 1948, especially after the Egyptian *coup d'état* of July 1952, and the rise of President Jamal Abdel Nasser, Egyptian universities were open to Arab students at no charge. This was an excellent opportunity for thousands of Palestinian students to attend Egyptian universities, causing a great educational boom. Many poor students were able to attend college and choose any specialization they were qualified for.

After 1967, a good number of universities were established in the West Bank and Gaza. Their students, as mentioned above, would become the sparks that ignited resistance against the Zionist occupation.

As a result of the 1948 Nakba, UNRWA (United Nations Refugees and Work Agency) was set up and their schools played a great role in making education available for the children of Palestinian refugees. The curriculum followed at the UNRWA schools in Jerusalem and the rest of the country, both on the West and East Banks of Jordan, was that of the Jordanian Ministry of Education. For a short period of time after 1967, I supervised the health care service given to UNRWA schools in Jerusalem. We formed health awareness committees to take care of the cleanliness of the refugee camps in Jerusalem.

The Suffering of the Children of Palestine

After the 1967 occupation of the West Bank and Gaza, and especially after the two intifadas, the standard of education went downhill as a result of the savage behavior of the occupation army. Long curfews were imposed, schools and universities were closed, and teachers and students were arrested. Some schools were physically occupied by the army and turned into military barracks. All these factors disrupted education. According to a report by the UN High Commission, the violence committed by the Israeli Army has caused both psychological and social problems among young pupils. This cruel policy caused disruption to all aspects of life of the population, causing suffering not only to children and young people but also to the whole society.

PART TWO

Franciscan monks in Jerusalem (c. 1905)

7.
Religions

IN THE YEAR 636 (15 HIJRI), the Muslim Caliph 'Umar Ibn al-Khattab, in a most humble manner, entered Jerusalem and received its keys from the city's Orthodox Patriarch, Sophronius, to whom he gave what was called *al-'Uhda 'l-'Umariyya* (the Umariyya Covenant). This covenant granted security to the people of Jerusalem—their lives, churches, crosses, and wealth—provided that they paid taxes the way other cities did, and did not allow "Byzantians and thieves" to remain in the city. It also granted security to those who wished to leave the city until they could reach their secure destination. At the request of the people of Jerusalem, the covenant promised to not allow Jews to live in their city. Those citizens of Jerusalem who had chosen to leave with the Byzantians were allowed to come back, provided that they abide by the laws accepted by the rest of the people of Jerusalem. The following is a translation of the text of this covenant:

> In the name of God, the most Merciful, the most Compassionate. This is what the servant of God, 'Umar Ibn al-Khattab, amir al-mu'minin (the commander of the faithful) has granted to the people of Aelia (Capitolina) as an assurance of security (aman). He has granted them protection for their lives, their possessions, their churches and crosses. This applies to both the sick and the healthy and to the rest of their religious community. Their churches are not to be taken over, nor to be destroyed or reduced in number or size; neither will their crosses and their possessions. They are not to be forced to change their religion, nor is any one of them to be harmed. No Jews are to live with them in Aelia.

Like the people of other cities, it is required of the people of Aelia to pay the jizya [tax]. It is also required of them to oust Byzantians and thieves. Those who leave the city are granted security for their lives and wealth until they reach their secure destination. Those who choose to stay are granted protection and have to pay jizya the same as the rest of the people of Aelia. Those of the people of Aelia who wish to leave with the Byzantians and carry their wealth with them, abandoning their churches and crosses are given security for their lives, commerce and children until they reach their secure destination. Outsiders who have taken refuge in the city and wish to stay, may do so provided they pay jizya the way the people of Aelia do; while those of them who wish to leave with the Byzantians may do so. Those who decide to come back to their people will not have any taxes levied on them until they harvest their crops. This is a guarantee in the name of God given by the caliphs and the faithful, as long as they [the people of Aelia] pay their jizya.

Written and passed on the 15th year after Hijr, and witnessed by Khalid ibn al-Walid, 'Abd al-Rahman ibn 'Awf, 'Amr ibn al-'As, and Mu'awiya ibn Abi-Sufyan.

Ever since this covenant, Muslims and Christians in Jerusalem have lived together peacefully, a kind of coexistence that does not exist in many other places in the world. There was one exception to this coexistence between different sects. During the period between 1099 and 1187, European Crusaders occupied the city and committed atrocities not only against Muslims, but also against Orthodox Christians. It is interesting that the Muslims had always respected Christian churches, while the Christian Crusaders occupied or destroyed the churches of the Orthodox Christians.

After Salah al-Din al-Ayyubi (Saladin) liberated Jerusalem from the clutches of the Crusaders on 2 October 1187, peaceful coexistence between Muslims and Christians was restored and remained so until today. Even when Jews started to come in small numbers to live in Jerusalem, religious tolerance was observed in the city. Turmoil in Jerusalem and the rest of Palestine was a natural result of the threat to the status quo by the influx of Zionist Jews into Palestine after 1918.

In the middle of the 19th century, Western consuls in Jerusalem had an increased influence in the city, and they granted Palestinian Christians special privileges. As a result, the number of churches and monasteries increased, together with an increase in the number of schools that were connected to those monasteries. Still, the peaceful relationship between Muslims and Christians remained unchanged. Many Christian families in the Old City, in a friendly gesture, but sometimes in a sincere belief, used to fast alongside their Muslim neighbors during the month of Ramadan. As people started to move from their old houses in the Old City, many customs ceased to be observed, but good relations between Muslims and Christians continued. Muslims and Christians shared many activities, especially in the realm of cultural societies, where religion had nothing to do with qualifications for membership. At the end of the 19th century and the beginning of the 20th century, literary societies gained wide popularity. The most important was *al-Adab al-Zahira*, chaired by Dawood al-Saydawi.

Political parties and societies began to be established in 1918 to defend the country against the danger of Zionism, especially after the British occupation of Southern Syria (Palestine and East-Jordan today). Zionism was seen as targeting both Muslims and Christians and the new associations united Muslims and Christians. Some societies had the cross inside the crescent as their emblem expressing Muslim-Christian solidarity. The most active political party in Palestine, the Higher Arab Committee, chaired by Hajj Amin al-Husaini, was established in Jerusalem by prominent Muslim and Christian figures in the wake of the General Strike of 1936.

Characterized by a great procession to a holy site located on the way to Jericho from Jerusalem, al-Nabi Musa festival was very important for Palestinians, both Muslims and Christians. On April 2, 1920, following custom and carrying the traditional flags, a great crowd started the march from al-Aqsa Mosque, after being bid farewell by the notables of Jerusalem. For the first time in Palestinian history, a religious fight took place between Muslim and Christian Arabs, on one side, and immigrant European Jews, on the other side, as a result of a hand grenade that a Jewish person had thrown into the middle of the crowd. Speakers, both Christian and Muslim, made rousing speeches urging people to stand together in defense of their homeland against British imperialism and Zionist colonial immigration.

At the beginning of the 20th century, the people of Jerusalem were religious and conservative, and they were keen that their children absorbed religious and traditional ethics.

Christian families kept icons in their houses representing the Virgin Mary and Jesus Christ, as well as some of the prominent saints. Children used to accompany their parents to church on Sundays and other religious occasions, as well as to weddings. Those habits were observed until the 1948 disaster took place, after that they began to diminish.

Muslim families had their children learn the Holy Qur'an bit by bit until the whole book was completed, at which occasion, as described above, a great celebration was held. Together with pictures of the Holy Kaaba and al-Aqsa Mosque, the walls in Muslim houses were decorated with verses from the Qur'an in beautiful decorative Arabic calligraphy. Daily prayers were performed in front of children so that they would become used to them and observe them as they grew up. Fasting during the month of Ramadan was fully observed in the cities and villages alike. On the first night of Ramadan, villagers had the habit of strewing seven kinds of seeds—wheat, barley, maize, vetch, millet, lentils, and kidney beans—at the entrance of their homes. Sometimes, table salt was also added. This was believed to exorcise evil spirits. In the same way they learned to pray at a young age, children also learned to fast during the month of Ramadan. Children loved this month because it was an occasion of special customs for children, like collecting whatever sweets and snacks they could get during the daytime, to enjoy in the evening after breaking their fast. An old Turkish cannon at the upper level of al-Sahera Graveyard used to be fired to mark the end of the fast and the time to break the fast, which happens at sunset during Ramadan. This cannon was a source of great joy for children. Children would climb a high place, like a house roof, to be able to see and hear the cannon or hear the *adhan* (call for prayers) from the nearest mosque. Then they would run back home to tell their parents that it was time to break the fast. The whole family would take their meal together.

Children used to consider fasting during Ramadan a sacred matter that should not be violated. Children would ask their friends if they were fasting and to prove it by showing their tongue, for a dry tongue was proof of fasting. If a child was not fasting, the other children would sing a mocking song that goes:

> You who are not fasting in Ramadan
> You're belittling your religion
> Our black cat will take out your intestines!

In addition to the main course, the traditional Ramadan table contained special food and drink that were meant to enhance the appetite, like drinks made from licorice, carob, and tamarind; hummus; a salad called *fattoush*; and various kinds of pickles. The main course is a hot dish rich in rice, vegetables, and meat. Until today, people have kept the habit of breaking their fast by taking a date and a glass of either water or one of the drinks mentioned above. Special Ramadan sweets, the most famous of which is called *qatayef*, are taken at the end of the meal. A short prayer is read before breaking the fast. Very religious people would perform their full Maghreb prayers immediately after breaking their fast with dates and water, then would come back to take their meal. Children were always keen on finishing their meal quickly to be able to go out to play in the street. The evenings of Ramadan were full of various activities that brought pleasure to all members of the family.

Nowadays, as is to be expected, many Ramadan customs have changed. The radio and television have obviated the firing of the cannon, the refrigerator takes away the need to buy cold drinks, hummus, and *qatayef* just before the time to break the fast. Fatty dishes are being avoided for health reasons and various rich dishes are being avoided for economic reasons.

From the dawn of Islamic history, it has been tradition to have a recital of the Holy Qur'an at al-Aqsa Mosque during the month of Ramadan. Prominent readers of the Qur'an from the whole Arab and Islamic world took part in this ritual. Al-Aqsa Mosque is one of the three holiest Islamic shrines; the other two being the great Mosque of Mecca and the Mosque of the Prophet at Medina. At the dawn of Islam, when the shrine at Mecca was filled with the idols worshipped by the non-Muslim Arabs, the early Muslims were ordered to pray facing the direction of al-Aqsa in Jerusalem. Hence, Jerusalem was named the first *qibla*. Before the Israeli occupation of Jerusalem in 1967, most of the famous readers of the Qur'an came from Egypt, Syria, and Lebanon. Mustafa Isma'il, and 'Abd al-Basit 'Abd al-Samad, both from Egypt, and Salah Kubbara, from Lebanon, used to attract hundreds of listeners with their beautiful voices and perfect recitations. After the occupation, this ritual continued by local readers. During Ramadan, al-Aqsa Mosque becomes an even greater point of attraction for many Muslims, whether from Jerusalem or other cities. People liked to observe the *'Isha* (evening) prayers at this holy mosque, followed by the *Tarawih* prayers that are a particular feature of Ramadan.

After observing these prayers, people would normally go out to visit their relatives, a habit that is highly recommended in Islam for its positive effect in strengthening family ties. Such family visits during Ramadan had a special flavor, as visiting men brought with them a basket full of fruit, both fresh and dried, as well as local sweets. As the whole family used to take part in this kind of visit, one generation after another adopted this custom. Children used to enjoy these visits a great deal, as it was a chance to enjoy the various kinds of sweets and the special treatment usually given to children. Aside from such visits, men would also spend a good part of Ramadan evenings in cafés, busying themselves with playing cards and backgammon. In certain cafés, a *hakawati* would be hired to entertain the audience by reciting traditional old Arab epics, like *'Antara* and *Abu-Zayd al-Hilali*. The *hakawati* is an eloquent man who told tales to the audience taken from traditional Arab folklore, partly based on real events from history about old Arab heroes, and partly enriched and embellished by fictional episodes. Telling such tales was quite an art, as the *hakawati* had to color his language and accent in such a way as to excite his audience. When I was a child, a man called Sheikh Salih Khamis was the most famous *hakawati* in Jerusalem. The most important cafés where *hakawatis* performed in Jerusalem during our time were Muna, Za'tara, Bab al-Mafariq, and Bab Hutta. Radio and television have spoiled many of these traditional customs.

Both the elders and the youngsters also enjoyed *karakuz 'owaz*, the shadow theater.

Women remained at home while the men went to cafés, and they entertained themselves by visiting or receiving their neighbors. Together they would spend the evenings either performing rituals, like reading *al-Sira al-Nabawiyya* (the Prophet's biography), or singing and playing the *oud* and the tabla.

A prominent figure at the marketplace in the evenings was the licorice vendor, with his ornamented large brass container that he carried by means of a strong band around his shoulder. Around his waist, he also carried a rounded brass holder for mugs. Fixed on his fingers were two small pieces of brass, called *faqqashat*, and with his beautiful voice delicately in tune with the rhythm of the *faqqashat*, he would call out to attract buyers for his delicious refreshing drink. Other vendors of various snacks and sweets, like nuts, beans, ice-cream, and *haris* were also there, roaming the city alleyways and calling out their wares in tuneful cries that particularly attracted children.

Children were the most joyful in the evenings of Ramadan, because they were allowed to go out to the nearby quarters. They were not afraid of going out in the evenings of Ramadan, as they believed that the wicked demons hid away during this holy month and it was only angels who flew around the place. They also had their own Ramadan songs that they chanted in the darkened alleys of the city. In their procession, together with the bags where they kept the sweets they had collected during the day, they would carry small handmade paper lanterns with candles inside. These candles were made out of orange peals after removing the edible part. The words of their songs were mostly taken from religious traditions. Groups of children would go from one house to another chanting to the other children to join them. They would then be well received and given traditional sweets and snacks. At the end of the evening, children would return home carrying the sweets and snacks they had collected, and they would remind their parents to wake them up for *suhur*, the meal taken before dawn as a preparation for fasting. For this meal, a man, called a *musahher*, used to roam the streets beating his drum and chanting to call people to wake up. The *musahher* gave special treatment to those who would give him '*eidiyya*, a financial gift, at the end of Ramadan, calling them by name and making sure they woke up. Every quarter of the city had its own *musahher*. The most famous in Jerusalem in my time was Adham Tiro, who used to know most of the people of Jerusalem and called them by name. On the day of the 'Eid, the *musahher* would make a round of the city houses to collect his '*eidiyya*. People, in turn, were generous with him. The *suhur* meal is a light one, with the kind of food that is supposed to help against the feeling of hunger or thirst. These traditions stopped after the 1967 Israeli occupation of Jerusalem, as it became dangerous for people to go out at night. Due to the occupation, the old spiritual atmosphere in Jerusalem has almost vanished.

During Ramadan, social peace prevailed as people remember the fact that fasting is not accepted by God unless people observe good conduct. In Islam, the idea of fasting is not simply abstaining from eating and drinking, it is also a symbol of ethical and spiritual ideals, such as abstaining from misbehaving and suppressing one's materialistic desires. In Jerusalem, those people who did not fast during Ramadan, like Christians, would respect the tradition and abstain from eating, drinking, or smoking in public. During the day, most cafés and restaurants would close down during Ramadan and open only in the evening. Ramadan was also the month of good deeds. Every family was supposed to give away a reasonable amount of money or food material, called *futra*, to the poor. Poor families who, in spite of their need, never asked for help were usually known to society and were the recepients of *futra*, which must be given away before the end of Ramadan.

On most Fridays, but especially during the holy month of Ramadan, the vast precincts of al-Aqsa would be full of worshippers who came from all over the country, as well as from neighboring Arab countries, to observe the main Friday prayers. Many religious people would spend the last ten days of Ramadan at al-Aqsa, and before the Israeli occupation, many pilgrims going to Mecca used to include Jerusalem in their pilgrimage. The 27th night of Ramadan is called *Laylat al-Qadr*, and special rituals are performed on this night. On the last Friday of Ramadan, called *al-Jum'a 'l-Yatima* (the last Friday), even greater numbers of worshippers would observe their Friday prayers at al-Aqsa. Despite the security measures imposed on Jerusalem by the occupying authorities, in 1999 about 250,000 people from all over the country marched to al-Aqsa to attend *al-Jum'a 'l-Yatima* prayers. This was one of the greatest efforts that Palestinians made to demonstrate their adamant adherence to their traditions and resistance to the occupation.

Sufis also had their Ramadan rituals at one of the mosques or in their homes. A few men, after reading verses from the Qur'an and chanting songs in praise of Prophet Muhammad, stood in a circle and moved at the rhythm of a drum, chanting the name of Allah. Their movement and chanting gradually increased with the heightened rhythm of the drum until they reached a peak of total spiritual submission, at which time the leader stopped and the other men would do the same.

Commercial activity also increased during Ramadan, as people from the smaller towns and villages came to Jerusalem to buy their food and other merchandise and sell their produce. On the last day of Ramadan, the marketplace became particularly congested with people, as this is the day before 'Eid al-Fitr (the feast of breaking the fast). The same busy market happened on the day before 'Eid al-Adhha (the feast of the pilgrimage). Villagers flooded the city to buy clothes and sweets in particular, while others came to buy meat or have a haircut. Most people waited for that day to buy new clothes and shoes. This meant that tailors, shoemakers, and hairdressers had to spend the whole night before the day of the 'Eid finishing their customers' orders. Higher fees were expected for the occasion. The same held true for sweet makers who stayed up the whole night in order to complete the many orders for 'Eid sweets (*ma'mul* and *baqlawa*). In addition to men and boys getting a haircut, everybody took a bath for the 'Eid. Adults took a bath early in the morning on the 'Eid day before the *Fajr* (dawn) and the 'Eid prayers, whereas children were given a bath the day before. In the past, taking a bath was done the old fashioned way. Water would be heated in a large tin on a kerosene burner. Then, with a can, hot water would be mixed in a bucket with cold water until it was warm and bearable. From this bucket, water was ladled into a can and poured on the head and body. Soap was a local soap, made of pure olive oil and manufactured mainly in the city of Nablus, which was famous for this industry. Children were extraordinarily happy to have their 'Eid bath, thinking that 'Eid would not accept them unless they took a bath.

Joyful children used to keep their new clothes and shoes under their pillows and wake up early in the morning to put them on. The first thing they expected from their parents and other family members was the *'eidiyya*, a small amount of money given to them to spend on sweets and enjoying special 'Eid entertainment. Happily waiting for 'Eid the next day, children used to express their joyful feeling with special songs like this one:

> Tomorrow is our 'Eid that we'll celebrate
> By slaying the cow of Sayyed
> But Sayyed has no cow
> So we'll slay his blond daughter!

The day before 'Eid, women exerted a lot of effort to prepare their family and house for the occasion. A whole day would be spent cleaning almost every little thing in the house, otherwise, as the saying went, the 'Eid would refrain from entering the house! The bedcovers were washed, and the floor was cleaned with water and soap. In addition, special 'Eid cakes, called *ma'mul*, were usually prepared at home and sent to the public bakery to be baked, for house ovens were still unavailable. In spite of the fact that preparing *ma'mul* at home was quite tiring, it was shameful to buy it readymade from the *souq*. Women prided themselves on their ability to make it perfectly and when *ma'mul* was presented to the guests, eating some and showing appreciation were necessary compliments that the guests had to give to the homemaker, who otherwise might feel insulted. In the past, women neighbors gathered together to prepare 'Eid cakes and other food. Nowadays, such cakes are bought readymade from the *souq*, with no embarrassment, unless a homemaker wants to show her skills in making them.

In addition to offering sweets to the guests on 'Eid, some sweets were given away to needy people, in the name of dead family members. This custom, thought to be of pharaonic origin, is believed to make the souls of the dead rest in peace. Usually women went to the cemetery where their relatives were buried, carrying the sweets they intended to give away. There they read some verses of the Holy Qur'an for the souls of the dead and gave away the sweets to needy people who gathered at the cemetery for that purpose. Some people would ask a "reader" to recite the whole of the Qur'an or parts of it at the graveyard. These "readers" were not learned people, and many of them were blind. Since they had learned to recite the Holy Qur'an by heart, they would use this ability to earn some money on religious occasions like this.

On the day of 'Eid, family members would wake up early in the morning to be ready for a long day full of activities. Married people would take a bath and attend *al-Fajr* (dawn) prayers. Children, with their new clothes, would kiss the hands of their elderly relatives, who would give them each their *'eidiyya*, as mentioned above. Men went with their grown-up sons to a nearby mosque, but preferably to al-Aqsa Mosque, to pray the 'Eid prayers, which always have a special flavor. On their way to and from the mosque, they would stop every now and then to shake hands with other people who filled the streets, reciprocating good wishes for the festival. With special phrases that the crowd of people in the mosque uttere together, 'Eid prayers had a strong spiritual effect on the worshippers. When the prayers were over, people in the mosque shook hands with each other and exchanged good wishes. Beggars usually waited outside the mosque to get money from worshippers who were in the mood to give on the occasion of 'Eid.

After the praying rituals were observed, men left the mosque for the cemetery to visit the graves of their dead relatives where they would read some verses from the Holy Qur'an and ask God to be merciful with the dead. Visiting the graveyard, as mentioned above, is believed to be a pharaonic habit that some orthodox Muslims think of as a bad habit. But the majority of people still follow it. After that, men proceeded to visit their close relatives, particularly women. This is called silat al-rahm, and it is an old Arab-Islamic tradition followed by men to maintain good relationships with their women relatives. Seen as a token of protection, it made women, especially those married to men from another family, feel that their male relatives were there to protect them. In the old times, young women used to give respect to their old relatives by kissing their hands, a habit that has almost vanished. These visiting elders used to give 'eidiyya to their female relatives. Children accompanying their fathers loved these visits, as it was a chance for them to see and play with their cousins, as well as enjoy eating the 'Eid sweets offered to them. At noon, the head of the family came home from a tiring, but satisfying trip with the feeling of having done his duty toward his relatives.

In case grown-up sons lived in separate houses, they started their day by coming to their father's house to accompany him to 'Eid prayers, then to visit their aunts, kiss their hands, and give each her 'eidiyya. In the same way the head of the family visited his married sisters and daughters, his in-laws did the same by visiting his wife and giving her and her children their 'eidiyyas.

Lunch was the most important meal on the 'Eid day, and all the family would take it together. For the rich, stuffed lamb was the special food for this occasion. In the past, the lamb was purchased a few days before 'Eid and kept in the yard. Early in the morning on the day of 'Eid, a butcher came to slay the lamb and prepare it for the homemaker to cook. Usually the whole lamb was cooked in a large pot using two or three gasoline burners.

Traditionally, the table on which food was served (*tabliyya*), had very short legs, and people sat next to it on the floor. The family head, even today, has the task of carving the meat and distributing it among his family members. Some families, especially when their number was too large for the table to accommodate everyone, followed the custom of the men eating together first, followed by women and children.

With this meal, the 'Eid rituals and duties came to an end and the children were allowed to go out to play with their friends, spending whatever money they had collected. Elders continued to visit their relatives and friends throughout the days of the festival. Believing it a religious duty, some women prioritized visiting their dead relatives' graves. Still, even at the cemetery, women enjoyed this outing, where they read texts from the holy book, distributed sweets among beggars, and spend time chatting together. In the evening, when the men went out, women gathered together at one of their homes and spent the evening singing and dancing.

Naturally, children and young people enjoyed 'Eid the most. In addition to the pleasure of taking leave from school and being the greatest consumers of the many kinds of sweets, snacks, and drinks that were sold everywhere in the streets, children had the rare chance of going to a park near al-Aqsa where they rode primitive swings for a small amount of money. Older boys would hire bicycles and roam the streets and yards. Teenagers would go to the only cinema in Jerusalem in the 1930s, the Regent Cinema at the German Colony, where one could see two movies for the cost of one ticket. Their favorite movies were those of *Tarzan* and *Flash Gordon*. The Jewish immigrants had more cinemas, but Arabs rarely attended them. Another activity for older teenagers was taking excursions to places near Jerusalem, like Wadi al-Qalt, 'Ain Fara, or Ramallah.

Girls, however, were less lucky, as they never had the freedom granted to boys. They either accompanied their mothers or played with other girls at home.

On the last day of 'Eid, after three tiring days full of activities, children would prepare themselves, sadly perhaps, to go back to school. On this occasion, they used to sing:

> The joy of 'Eid has gone
> And the teacher's stick has come!

There are two major Muslim feasts: *'Eid al-Fitr* and *'Eid al-Adhha*. The former comes right after Ramadan and is enjoyed more because it is the celebration of the end of fasting. *'Eid al-Adhha* comes two months later, on the day the pilgrims perform their major rituals in Mecca. Except for using the same clothes bought new for *'Eid al-Fitr*, all rituals and customs apart from those related to the pilgrimage (*hajj*) were the same as in *'Eid al-Fitr*. *'Eid al-Adhha* involved sacrificing a lamb. Many of the families did not eat even a portion of the sacrificed lamb, as they preferred to distribute all its meat among the poor.

Jerusalem has a profound sacred value for Muslims. It is linked to a great event in Islam because it is the departure point of *al-Isra'*, the night journey. From Jerusalem, the Prophet Muhammad was carried to Heaven where he met with the prophets and messengers of God. The Prophet Muhammad's ascent to Heaven is called *al-Mi'raj*. The occasion of *al-Isra'* and *al-Mi'raj* is still celebrated on the 27th day of the month of *Rajab* every *Hijri* year. In addition, as mentioned above, before the great mosque of Mecca was cleaned of the idols that were worshipped by the infidels, al-Aqsa Mosque was the first *qibla*. Jerusalem is one of the three holiest cities in Islam, after Mecca and Medina.

Songs in praise of the Prophet Muhammad were much in vogue in Jerusalem and were recited particularly at al-Aqsa Mosque on almost all occasions. It is believed that their popularity increased as Arabs felt the fall of their status when foreigners dominated the political scene in the Islamic state. They were interpreted as a kind of resistance against being dissolved by non-Arab dominant nations. That is why most of those songs emphasized the fact that Prophet Muhammad was an Arab. These songs, recited to beautiful tunes, were sometimes accompanied by body movements similar to those of the Sufis. Many men and women in Jerusalem were noted for their reciting abilities. The most popular occasion for such recitals was the birthday of the Prophet on the 12th day of the month of *Rabi' al-Awwal* according to the Hijri calendar. The following few lines are taken from a long poem sung in praise of Prophet Muhammad:

> O, people of the right path
> Make your prayers in the name of the Prophet
> The finest of the finest
> Who traveled by night
> And came back before dawn
> Congratulations, O, Halima[10]
> For being honored with His shining face
> Out of His widespread merits
> You are assured of salvation
> Thank God who'd revealed out of the bride's forehead a dawn full of light

Some songs in praise of the Prophet were also sung at weddings and similar occasions. The following are a few lines taken from a long poem that was sung by the late Sheikha Zahra Al-Salih, the most famous woman in Jerusalem at her time. She sang while majestically sitting on a high podium, her pretty face radiant with joy. This famous poem, called *al-Jawzi*, was sung for brides:

> Who raised in their perfect orbits a sun and a shining moon
> Who chose the master of the two worlds, the beloved and bright Messenger
> Who gave him the assurance of respect to all His creatures.

Special sweets were also distributed on the occasion of the prophet's birthday. In Islamic convention it was recommended that men visit their close female relatives in the tradition of *silat al-rahm*.

The other occasion for praise songs was the new Hijri year on the first of Muharram, an occasion when people would hang a green olive branch at their doors, expressing their hope for a green, healthy, and wealthy year. The first of Muharram had been the beginning of the fiscal year until the British changed it to January 1 when they occupied the country after winning World War I. Despite this, house rents are still collected on 1 *Muharram*. For the Shiites, the

10th day of *Muharram*, called *'Ashura*, is the saddest occasion, for it is the anniversary of Imam Al-Hussein ibn Ali's martyrdom. Shiites gathered together at the house of one of their prominent men and performed a special ritual, beating themselves on their faces and chests, a sign of repentance for not having protected him enough in the battle in which he was martyred. Sweets were distributed for the soul of the "Master of all Martyrs." In fact, all Muslims, whether Sunni or Shiite, considered this occasion a sad day, and even now a special kind of sweet, called *'Ashura*, is prepared at home and distributed among poor people.

The *hajj*, or Muslim pilgrimage to Mecca, is one of the five pillars of Islam. People longed to carry out this obligation that was full of spiritual enjoyment, but also full of exhaustion and danger. Preparation for the *hajj* started several months before departure and if the trip was by land pilgrims would gather together in a caravan that was protected by armed guards. Another alternative was going by sea from Jaffa through the Suez Canal to Jeddah. Travel by sea was more secure, except for fear of disease and the usual dangers of sea travel. Land travel was dangerous due to road robbers and the possibility of being lost in the desert. That is why pilgrims were considered lost until they made it safely back home where they were considered reborn. Pilgrims had to take with them what they needed for sleeping, food, and water. Some took merchandise to sell in the Holy Land and on their way back brought other merchandise to sell at home. The pilgrimage caravan used to gather together at the city entrance or at al-Aqsa Mosque. All the city notables, relatives, and practically everybody in town would excitedly bid farewell to the pilgrims. Some would even escort the caravan to a distance outside the city. This was again an occasion for chanting the usual songs in praise of the Prophet, with words that referred to the sites visited in the Holy Land. The following lines are a good example:

> O you, who are leaving for Mina
> So much you've excited my heart
> As you march with your guide
> How lonely I feel after you

> In the name of God I beseech you
> When you visit Muhammad's grave
> Convey to him my hearty regards

Due to the near impossibility of maintaining contact with those who left, relatives worried until the pilgrims came back. The only means of contact were telegrams from Mecca or Medina, which mostly carried bad news. When news was received that the returning pilgrimage caravan was approaching the city, flocks of people would run to the city suburbs to receive the pilgrims with music and songs. The quarter to which one or more of the pilgrims belonged would be ornamented with lights and drawings and people would gather to welcome the returning pilgrims. In the way of social cooperation, people brought gifts that were likely to help the pilgrims give refreshment to their guests, like rice, sugar, and coffee. Pilgrims, on the other hand, would bring with them various gifts, the most important being a small amount of water taken from Zamzam Well in Mecca.[11] A sip of this holy water was offered to the welcoming guests, together with dates from the Holy Land as a blessing. The kernel of the date would be kept in one's pocket as a good omen for prosperity. As can be expected, the returning pilgrim would happily spend time describing the details of his journey to the eager guests. Women pilgrims would do the same, except that they would make it more enjoyable by having a reader of *al-Sira al-Nabawiyya* (the Prophet's biography) and chanting the religious *muwashahat* (songs with special rhythm and rhyme). The most popular song was the one that the people of Yathreb (Medina) received the Prophet with when he emigrated from Mecca to their town (September 24, 622), the words of which are:

> The full moon has risen
> From behind the turn of al-Wada'
> Being grateful is our duty
> So long as someone calls for submission to God
> You who has been chosen messenger [of God]
> We do submit to your call
> You have enlightened our town[12]

> And you, best of preachers, are most welcome

In the past, pilgrims, both during and after their pilgrimage, had to behave piously by observing their prayers and refraining from any behavior that might tarnish their pilgrimage. Men, especially elders, would let their beards grow and wear a white or colored turban and a traditional Arab cloak, called *'abah*. This made them look solemn and dignified. A woman pilgrim would wear a white shawl that hid her hair.

As people now travel safely and quickly in the luxury of airplanes and air-conditioned buses, these customs have changed in many ways. With modern travel facilities, more and more people are carrying out the pilgrimage every year. Following the Israeli occupation in 1967, more and more young people in Palestine became observant of Islam and its traditions. This is thought to be related to the belief that Palestine's defeat was a direct result of its people's laxness in their religion.

On the grounds that there should be no mediation between man and his Creator, there is no priesthood in Islam. However, because life is complicated, Muslims needed those who could explain to them the rules and regulations of their religion. This task, in Islamic history, was given to the judges, because they were the most knowledgeable in Islamic theology. Until the Ottomans rose to power, judges had no special dress. During the time of the Ottomans, judges and *'ulama* (theologians) wore a special cloak with a head turban that differed from one country to another. Because al-Aqsa Mosque has a sacred status for Muslims, it has always been served by highly learned *'ulama*, mostly graduates of al-Azhar in Cairo, working as *imams* (prayer leaders), *khatibs* (Friday preachers), or *faqihs* (jurists). In addition, there are other people, called *sadanah* (supporters), whose job is to take care of the mosque. The *khatib* of al-Aqsa Mosque, as well as the theologians attached to it, were very highly respected. A few well-known Jerusalem families had members who held the post of *khatib* at al-Aqsa. The post of *mufti*, the theologian who delivers a theological-legal opinion on major matters in Muslim life, was given equal respect.

There are also a few families in Jerusalem today who are remote descendents of the Prophet Muhammad through his only daughter, Fatima. They are called *ashraf*.

During the British Mandate, the Higher Islamic Council was responsible for all Islamic matters in Jerusalem and Palestine, including *awqaf* (religious endowments). After the Israeli occupation, the Department of *Awqaf* was in charge of al-Aqsa Mosque and the services appertaining to it. Israeli authorities tried many times to impose hegemony over this holy mosque, but they always encountered great resistance. However, the Israelis confiscated a large amount of funds intended for the mosque. Today, the excavations done by Israelis beneath al-Aqsa Mosque in a desperate search for the remains of the Temple of Solomon endangers the structure of the mosque and peace in the region. Nothing so far has been found. In fact, in the whole of Palestine, no ancient Jewish ruins have been found. Indeed, there is a group of archeologists and historians who believe that the ancient Jews had no connection with Palestine. As was mentioned earlier, according to Whitelam, "ancient Israelite history is the domain of Religion or Theology and not of History."[13]

In Jerusalem, there were a few groups of Sufis who performed their rituals at places called *zawaya*, plural of *zawiya*, meaning a closed place or a place of worship. During the Ottoman era, the *zawiya* was called *takiyya*, where *darawish*, plural of *darwish*, performed their rituals. Later, *takiyya* became known as the place where free food was served to the poor and to strangers visiting the holy places. To the public, Sufi and *darwish* have the same connotation. However, Sufis do not accept this, as they consider themselves more spiritual philosophers than the *darawish*. Sheikhs of the various Sufi *tariqas* (ways) were highly respected by the Muslim public. Some of these sheikhs would perform magic tricks, called *makrumat* (miracles), like inserting a whole sword in the mouth without spilling a drop of blood. To the orthodox Muslim 'ulama, however, Sufism is considered heresy.

The *'imama* (turban) is an old Arab headdress that has many similar shapes. An old saying goes that *'imamas* are Arab crowns. In later years, especially during the Ottoman era, it started to imply a religious connotation. Many men in Jerusalem who had no proper education used to memorize the Holy Qur'an and wear *'imamas* for the purpose of making money from reciting verses of the Qur'an at graveyards, houses of the deceased, or similar venues. Unfortunately, irrespective of their ignorance, they were sometimes mistaken for *'ulama* and sought for advice on religious matters. Many of them were glad to give their opinion, which, in many cases, was far from correct. Some of them claimed the ability to cure diseases or prevent envy by making amulets. There was no legal way to control such people.

On the other hand, Christians had a clerical hierarchy, with special vestments that differed from one community to another and according to the status of the priest. All of them, however, wore a large cross on the chest. In official processions, a group of escorts marched in front. In Arabic they are called *qawwasa* (bowmen). Most, if not all, of them were Muslims. Originally, these guards, who until today are armed with swords, were appointed by Saladin in order to protect Christian patriarchs. Today, in addition to making sure that the road is clear for the patriarchal procession, they give the procession a solemn ceremonial appearance. This job is inherited among certain Muslim families.

In Jerusalem, and the whole of Greater Syria, the largest Christian sect is Greek Orthodox, whose followers are descendents of the ancient Christian Arab tribes of Greater Syria before the appearance of Islam. As Islam did not force followers of monotheistic religions to convert to Islam, the majority of Christian Arabs chose to adhere to their original religion. During the Crusader campaigns, Christian Arabs were notably strong allies of the Muslims against these invaders, who had the objective of "rescuing" Jerusalem from the clutches of the Muslims and the Christians of the Eastern Church. Today, all major Christian communities, namely Catholics, Protestants, Anglicans, Armenians, both Catholic and Orthodox, Assyrians, Maronites, Copts, and Ethiopians, are represented in Jerusalem.

Each community has a share in the Church of the Holy Sepulchre, the way they do at the Nativity Church of Bethlehem. That is why skirmishes sometimes occur between the various communities on certain matters, like who is responsible for cleaning the church. And that is why, from the time of the 'Umariyya Covenant, the keys to this major church have been entrusted to two Muslim families. The Joudeh family keeps the keys and the Nusseibeh family opens and closes the main and only entrance to the church. Every time the church is to be opened or closed, a representative of the Nusseibeh family takes the keys from the representative of the Joudeh family, opens or closes the gate of the church and returns the keys to the Joudeh family representative. The Israeli authorities tried to impose their hegemony over the church, to the extent of trying to open a new gate to the church, but they encountered great resistance. It is important to mention here that throughout history, Muslims have treated the Christian churches with great respect and no violation incident has been recorded. However, two years after the Israeli occupation of Jerusalem, on August 12, 1969, three Israelis stole the crown of the Virgin Mary from the Golgotha of the Church of the Holy Sepulchre. The next day, the Latin Patriarch issued a decree ordering the closure of the three churches in Jerusalem because of this sabotage by Israelis. Other assaults against churches also took place, such as the destruction of the Orthodox Church at Jabal al-Tour.

Ever since the advent of Islam, Christians and Muslims in Palestine have been strong allies. On no occasion, including during the Crusaders' invasion, have Arab Christians sided against their Muslim brothers. Today, they both work hand in hand to resist the Israeli occupation of Palestine. The societies that were formed in Palestine in the 1920s and after for the purpose of resisting Zionist Jewish immigration were all given the name "Muslim-Christian," to show that the followers of both faiths were united against this invasion. The philanthropic societies in Palestine, whether Muslim or Christian, have lent their help to all people, irrespective of their religion or sect.

Christian Feasts

Jerusalem is well-known for its numerous religious feasts and popular celebrations throughout the year. In a wholesome environment of rare tolerance, Muslims and Christians have always cooperated together in bringing these festivals to life.

In Jerusalem, there are about one hundred monasteries, with their twenty-four schools. In 1947, the Christian population amounted to 27,000, whereas in 1996, nineteen years after the Israeli occupation of the city, the number had decreased to only about 9,000. One fears that sometime in the future Jerusalem may turn into a museum visited only by tourists taking pictures of its empty churches and monasteries.

The most important Christian feasts, which may be celebrated by different denominations on different dates, are Palm Sunday, Good Friday, and Holy Saturday during Easter, which are officially celebrated in Jerusalem. Christmas has its main celebration in Bethlehem. In addition to these feasts, there are many others, like the feast of Our Lady the Virgin Mary and Holy Week. Palm Sunday refers to Jesus Christ's entrance into Jerusalem riding a donkey and the people receiving and welcoming him with palm fronds. The Catholics personify this event by following the steps taken by Jesus Christ from Bethany (the villageof al-'Aizariyya on the Mount of Olives, where the biblical Lazarus had lived and where he was raised from the dead by Christ) to Jerusalem (through the Old City's eastern St. Stephen's or Lions Gate). The Orthodox, on the other hand, organize a procession headed by the Patriarch and his entourage in their ceremonial vestments, followed by the city officials and notables, with children at the back of the parade, carrying palm fronds decorated with flowers and colored ribbons.

Via Dolorosa (Stations of the Cross)

It became a custom for some religious people, whether from Jerusalem or from outside the city, to carry a cross and reenact Jesus Christ's Way of the Cross on foot carrying crosses through the fourteen stations.

The Passion (Dolorous/Via Dolorosa) "Way of the Cross" has fourteen stations:
1. The point where Jesus Christ was crowned with a wreath of thorns (al-Rawdha and Zion's Nuns School).
2. The point where Jesus Christ was forced to carry the cross.
3. The point where Jesus Christ lost consciousness and fell down (at the crossroads between the al-Wad and Damascus Gate near the Catholic Armenian Monastery).
4. The point where Jesus Christ met his mother.
5. The point where Jesus Christ felt the heaviness of the cross and was about to fall down before Sam'an al-Qayrawani (Simon the Cyrenian) came to his help (at the place where al-Wad Road and al-Mufti Stairs meet).
6. The point at the Catholic Church that was the house of Saint Veronica, who mopped Jesus Christ's sweat from his forehead (near the Roman Catholic Church).
7. The point where Jesus fell for the second time (at the junction between the Via Dolorosa and Khan Al-Zayt).
8. The point where Jesus Christ addressed the crying women, "Do not cry for me, rather cry for your town that shall be doomed to destruction." (at Khanqa Stairs, near the Greek Roman Monastery).
9. The point where Jesus Christ fell with exhaustion under the heavy cross (near the eastern entrance of Coptic Monastery).
10-13. These stations are inside the Holy Church of the Holy Sepulchre near Golgotha (*al-Juljula*).
14. The point at the Holy Grave.

The Maundy Thursday

It is called the Holy Thursday and the Great Thursday, commemorating Jesus Christ washing the feet of his disciples. All Christian communities celebrate this occasion in their respective traditional ways at the site of the Holy Sepulchre, adjacent to the Mosque of Omar, named after the Muslim leader who declined to pray in the Sepulchre to preserve its Christian character. In a splendid scene that attracts thousands of Palestinian worshippers and pilgrims from around the world, and tourists interested in Palestinian culture and history, the Eastern Orthodox (Greek and Arab) reenact this event in the Sepulchre's Square in traditional slendor that would, centuries later, become Europe's religious dramas (eg. The Passion Play). The somber ceremony is reenacted on an elevated wood and wrought iron rectangular platform with twelve seats for "the Apostles" (represented by bishops) and one for Jesus Christ (rpresented by Jerusalem's Orthodox Patriarch). Reenacting Jesus Christ, the patriarch washes the feet of twelve Apostles (bishops) in an act of sincere humility dramatized by the arched back of the kneeling patriarch and the silence of the faithful, many of whom, showing signs of anguish as the patriarch pours water on each Apostle's feet and dries them with a cloth, rises and moves laboriously to the next Apostle. In the meanwhile, youngsters of the Orthodox sect celebrate the occasion on the roof of St. Jacob Church, chanting, playing the sword and shield (*sayf wa turs*) and dancing *dabka* (a folklore dance in vogue in Greater Syria).

Good Friday

This is a purely religious day consecrated for prayers only, following the fourteen stations of the Way of the Cross. At three o'clock in the afternoon, the time when Jesus Christ was crucified, a requiem is held, with special psalms following the Gregorian Mass. In the Eastern Orthodox church, the event is preceded by a slow, cadenced peel of the Sepulcher's large bell. Although the Holy Sepulchre was, prior to 1948, the focal point of this solemn event, most churches and monasteries in outlying areas participated in the event, attracting local communities. The attraction to the Holy Sepulchre was its trained choirs, the presence of large numbers of clergy representing various Christian denominations, and the ambience of the ancient church itself.

Holy Saturday

With the exception of the Catholic Church and a few others, nearly all Christian churches believe in the holy fire, the spiritual light emanating from the Holy Tomb without human intervention. All these communities—Armenian, Syrian, Coptic, and Ethiopian—have the tradition of receiving "light," symbolized by a burning candle, from the Greek Orthodox patriarch, who has been sequestered behind the sealed entrance of the Holy Tomb the night before. With this sacred light they bring light to their own churches.

The Orthodox patriarch inaugurates the celebration inside the Holy Tomb. After the Mass is over, government officials, accompanied by representatives of the Joudeh and Nusseibeh families, enter the grave to make sure that no combustible material has been there. Then they lock the door and an authorized person from the Joudeh family seals it. The door is kept sealed until the Greek Orthodox patriarch comes in at noon. In the meantime, processions of the various Eastern communities enter the church and take their designated places. Visitors and pilgrims also enter the place around the Holy Tomb and Golgotha (*al-Juljula*).

Balconies facing the Holy Tomb and overlooking Golgotha are reserved for the local governor and his family, the police commandant and his family, and to notables coming from Aleppo, Damascus, Lebanon, Jordan, and other neighboring places. After this internal organization, Greek Orthodox youngsters coming from the various towns and villages in the country are allowed to celebrate the occasion outside the church by marching in a parade, accompanied by drummers and dancers of the sword and shield dance, and chanting their special songs, like the following song:

> The Holy Saturday is our feast
> This is the order of our Master
> Our Master is Jesus Christ, our Savior
> With his blood he redeemed us
> Happy today we are
> And sad are the Jews

Meanwhile, the patriarch in his black cloak, comes out of the Patriarchate and enters the Holy Sepulchre and closes its gate. He kisses the sealed door of the Holy Tomb and opens it. Then, in front of the crowd, he takes off his clothes and dons a special white dress for the occasion and enters the Tomb alone. In the meantime, the

Orthodox *mukhtar* (representative) distributes the traditional 13 banners among the representatives of thirteen Orthodox families, who carry the banners and make three tours around the Holy Tomb in silence, then give back the banners to the *mukhtar*. The banners are kept at the Holy Sepulchre in locked closets until the next year. During these moments silence is complete among the attendants of the church who amount to about 20,000. The 13 traditional Orthodox families of Jerusalem are the following: Salman, al-Ajrab, al-Habash, al-Harami, al-Baghl, al-Qar'a, Shamma'a, Katan, Mahshi, Abu-Zakariya, Mansur, 'Allushiyya, and Abu-Shahla.

At 13:00 hours the bells inside the dome of the Holy Sepulture are rung. Then, representatives of the al-'Aqruq family ring the bell inside the Sepulchre, announcing emanation of the spiritual light. At this moment all other small bells are rung, with men chanting and women ululating (*zagharid*). Then immediately the Patriarch distributes the spiritual light, when a man from the Sliheet family being the first person to receive it. This man then gives a branch to a community priest and another to a representative of the Armenian community, who in turn passes it to the Copts, and the Ethiopians (*Habash*). Then he ties a branch of light with a long rope from the Dome's upper entrance windows over the Holy Tomb and pulls it with the light and goes out from a special door at the top of the dome leading immediately to the roof of the Greek Orthodox Monastery. In no time the light is spread, as everyone in the public uses it to light his or her candle. One of the funny traditions is that five persons from the community run fast in their white clothes over the shoulders of the public, carrying candles as if they were running on the floor. At the end, the crowd leaves the church with great difficulty, while youngsters gather together on the roof of the Greek Orthodox Monastery singing, dancing *dabka* and playing the sword-and-shield. Afterward they go to the Christian Quarter yard, where they continue their celebration.

It is worth mentioning here that at this time a crowd of Muslims from Jerusalem and its region gather at the yard of al-Aqsa Mosque preparing for the march to the site of Nabi Musa (Prophet Moses) Festival to celebrate and participate in the annual rituals.

Easter Sunday

This day is known as the "Descending of the Patriarch," as the Greek Orthodox Patriarch, in his sumptuous vestments, comes down, preceded by his clergy, and followed by the town notables. The parade moves toward the Church of the Holy Sepulchre, where the great Easter celebration takes place.

In other towns, the Easter Mass is performed on Sunday at dawn, after which people go out of the church leaving a man behind representing Satan. After prayers outdoors in the churchyard, a priest knocks on the church door saying three times: "Open up eternal doors, let the King of Glory come in!" Then the crowd enters the church chanting, "Jesus rose from among the dead!"

Easter celebrations, being the major Christian feast, go on for a week. What makes these celebrations most joyful for Jerusalem, however, is that they coincide with the Muslim celebrations during the Nabi Musa (Prophet Moses) season, which Saladin initiated after liberating Jerusalem from the clutch of Crusaders. This Islamic gathering takes place in Jerusalem before moving to the celebration site on the way to Jericho. Throughout history, no skirmishes have ever been seen between the two gatherings.

Children loved this feast, for its colored eggs and *ma'mul* (the popular local sweet).

What made this feast unique was the presence of great gatherings from outside Jerusalem, both Christian and Muslim. The merchants and hotel-keepers of Jerusalem benefited a lot from the tourists attending this and other feasts. Commercial activity, especially in the Old City markets, was enhanced by groups of Christians coming from Cyprus, Greece, Egypt, Syria, and Lebanon. In addition to this commercial activity, social life in the city was enlivened. Egyptian Copts used to rent houses or rooms in Jerusalem before, during, and after the feast and spent money on food and locally-made icons and crosses made of olive wood or mother-of-pearl. Egyptians in particular used to enliven the city atmosphere with their unique sense of humor. Cypriots came to the city in caravans and mostly belonged to the poorer class of society. They were known for buying used clothing. Syrians, Lebanese, and Iraqis typically stayed with their relatives in Jerusalem or the nearby towns, but some stayed at hotels.

After the Israeli occupation in 1967, however, tourism from Arab countries, as well as from Greece and Cyprus, ceased and the occupation authorities made life difficult for both Muslims and Christians in the city. As a result of the Israeli occupation, some of the Christian institutions and Holy Book libraries have closed down and the Christian population in Jerusalem has dramatically diminished. These factors have deprived the feasts of their old spiritual and joyful atmosphere, especially since celebrations have been reduced to a much smaller scale.

Many other festivals are celebrated by the various Christian churches, like those of Mar Elias and Mar Butrus. Such celebrations are performed at the church that carries the name of the celebrated saint. Prayers are read, then followed by popular festivals, smaller in scale than the festivities of the major feasts. The most important of these festivals are the following:

Ascension Day/Holy Thursday

This day is celebrated in memory of Jesus Christ ascending from the Mount of Olives to Heaven, forty days after Easter Sunday. The celebration starts with crowds of people marching to the Mount of Olives, singing songs that mingle with the echoes of church bells. A few churches, the largest of which is the Russian Church, rise over the top of this mountain that overlooks Jerusalem, the River Jordan, and the Dead Sea. At this place a number of Arab and Muslim martyrs from Umari and Ayyubi times have been buried.

Whitsunday/Pentecost

Fifty days after Easter, Christians celebrate this day on the Mount of Olives, in memory of the Holy Spirit's descent on the apostles of Jesus. The celebration continues for the whole day.

Holy Cross Day

This day is in memory of Queen Helena finding the cross believed to be the one on which Jesus Christ was crucified. Mass was held at the Cross Cave, located in the underground floor of the Church of the Holy Sepulchre. The popular celebration was held at al-Musallaba Monastery. People attending the celebration were allowed to move around the monastery and visit its valuable library. On this day people cook *muhammara* (roasted chicken with potatoes) and take their food outside Jerusalem to towns and villages where they celebrate with singing, dancing *dabka*, horse racing, and fencing. On the night of this feast, people burn wood as a symbol of saving the cross from the fire-worshipping Persians.

Mar Elias Feast

Mar Elias Greek Orthodox Monastery, one of the largest monasteries, is located about 4 miles (6 kilometers) south of Jerusalem in the direction of Bethlehem. Celebrations start one day before the feast, which occurs on July 20 every year, according to the Eastern Orthodox calendar. The singing and dancing on this feast are similar to other feasts.

Barbara Day

Youngsters wear masks on their faces and roam around the city quarters singing and dancing. People on this day cook *balila*, which is made from boiled wheat, sugar, almonds, walnuts, and sesame seeds.

Epiphany

On this night, people stay awake until midnight, believing that the gates of Heaven open up on this day and prayers will be answered. The priest passes by the houses to bless the followers of his church with holy water and they, in turn, drop money in his bucket. On this occasion, people eat *zalabiya*, a special kind of doughnut.

The official and public celebration used to take place at the River Jordan where Jesus Christ was baptized. A procession, headed by the archbishop, moved from Jerusalem to Mar Yohanna (St. John) Monastery, near the baptism place on the river. A mass, perhaps the strangest in Christian rituals, was held at the river. Together with some of the priests, the archbishop embarked on a boat floating in the river where the Mass is held. Then the archbishop dipped the cross in the river as a token of the baptism of Jesus Christ. At this moment, in a most beautiful and strange scene, thousands of pilgrims, watching on both banks of the river, carrying candles and wearing white robes, throw themselves into the water to be blessed. Women ululate *zagharid* and men dance *dabka*, while others sing the beautiful, traditional Byzantine psalm, "With your baptism, Our Lord, in River Jordan …" Particularly, Russian pilgrims, who used to make up a great number of the pilgrims before the communist revolution, kept their white robes to be used as their shrouds when they died.

After the 1967 Israeli occupation, the Epiphany celebratory events were curtailed. Also, the site of the celebrations changed to the eastern side of the River Jordan after the Jordanian Department of Archeology announced the discovery of the actual baptism site at Wadi al-Kharrab.

Christmas

Christmas is celebrated annually on December 25, according to the Western Calendar, and on January 7 or 14, according to the Eastern Calendar. Celebrations for Christmas started several weeks earlier, as people redecorated and beautified their shops and houses with special Christmas ornaments like the Christmas tree, and icons representing Jesus Christ, the Virgin Mary, together with a model of the stable where Jesus was born, and the three shepherds. Christmas hymns were heard in almost all the streets and alleys of Jerusalem, especially in *Haret al-Nasara* (the Christian Quarter). Christmas hymns sung by Fairuz, the most famous Lebanese singer, became in vogue after 1963. Parents took their children to the marketplace to buy them gifts and new clothes, and children enjoyed the story of Santa Claus.

Attended by high-ranking officials, the main official Christmas celebration took place at the Church of the Nativity in Bethlehem. Due to the resistance against Israeli occupation, however, a siege has been imposed on the city and the celebration is now predominantly religious.

Christmas Mass is held at midnight by the Orthodox Patriarch and by the Catholic Patriarch. At the Church of the Holy Sepulchre a smaller religious celebration is held. Christmas is a family feast, and families spend Christmas together and eat rich food, particularly chicken and turkey, as well as special sweets for the occasion.

New Year's Eve
Like everywhere else in the world, New Year's Eve was celebrated at hotels and public places by both Christians and Muslims, as well as by foreign visitors to the city. Rarely have any problems occurred as a result of people enjoying themselves during these celebrations. After the 1967 Israeli occupation, with the siege imposed on the occupied territories, as well as the tight economic situation, such celebrations became more difficult and almost impossible.

No special religious celebration is observed on the first day of the New Year. The head of the family used to bring home a sack filled with chestnuts, walnuts, almonds encrusted with sugar, and other sweets. *Kunafa* was always the sweet of choice at all occasions.

Jewish Celebrations and Festivals
With the help and protection of the European consuls, Jewish settlement in Jerusalem started in the middle of the 19th century. A Talmudic school was established, followed by a hospital and a synagogue. The number of settlers increased from a few individuals at the beginning of the century to about 10,000 before the British Mandate at the end of World War I. These Jews lived securely and without restriction in Arab houses that were rented from Jerusalem families in the al-Sharaf Quarter and its neighborhood in the Old City. Until 1917, Jews had 21 settlements outside the Old City. Being of European origin and of a different culture, these Jews did not mix

with Arabs, whether Muslim or Christian, except on a limited scale. Arabs did not take part in the Jewish feasts. Jews, as well, did not take part in the Muslim or Christian feasts. In spite of this, I became acquainted with the Jewish feasts, especially because my family lived in Sheikh Jarrah Quarter, which is located near the Me'a Shearim Jewish Quarter.

As the number of the European Jews increased and their activities became conspicuously dubious, the people of Palestine, in general, became apprehensive about their presence and immigration activity. After World War I and the Sykes-Picot Agreement between Great Britain and France, which stipulated the division of Greater Syria between the British and the French, it became clear to Arabs in general, and Palestinians in particular, that some plot was being hatched by the British and the European Jews in Palestine. This gave rise to a continuous and ever greater uprising by the Arabs of Palestine against the British Mandate and Zionist settlement in Palestine.

In principle, it was not easy for the people of Palestine, whether Muslim or Christian, to mix with Jewish settlers. For, in addition to the differences in culture mentioned above, Jews have very complicated religious restrictions. This relates to their food and social habits as well as their attitude towards non-Jews. Orthodox Jews do not eat food prepared by non-Jews. There are, of course, secular Jews who do not believe in nor abide by those restrictions. But the mentality that these restrictions have formed over the years made it difficult for Jewish settlers to socialize within their new environment. Perhaps, harboring the dangerous goal of establishing a Jewish state for themselves at the expense of the indigenous people of Palestine, they intentionally did not want to mix with the local society. A very small minority of Jews used to take part in Muslim or Christian feasts. In general, however, the relationship between Arabs, both Muslim and Christian, and Jews was on a small scale and mainly took place in commerce and medicine. Jews were known in the fields of money exchange and gold craft. Coming from Europe, there were a few renowned Jewish doctors.

Food habits followed by the Jews are very strict. Jews believe that man was created to eat food of plant origin only. After the great flood, however, God permitted man to eat flesh, albeit under strict rules. To start with, Jews are very strict in the conditions under which an animal is slain. Only a man of religion, called *shohat*, who is experienced in legal slaying, may slay an animal. Should a non-Jewish person touch the animal or the bird during the process of its slaying or before its blood is drained, that animal or bird is not allowed to be eaten by a Jew. There is a long list of specifications regarding the animals which may be eaten by Jews. Kosher food is also governed by many strict rules.

The Sabbath is a religious day for Jews and is strictly adhered to. This is a 24-hour holiday that starts at sunset on Friday afternoon and ends at sunset on Saturday afternoon. In conservative families, the woman of the house, before the Sabbath starts, lights at least two candles and prepares three meals that are placed on the table with two complete loaves of bread for each meal. There are many restrictions on what Jews may or may not do on the Sabbath, but these vary from one Jewish school of thought to another. It is generally accepted that Jews ask their non-Jewish neighbors to do for them what they are not allowed to do, like switching on the light at night. Needless to say that quarrels often occur between conservative and secular Jews when the latter do not abide by the Sabbath restrictions. Some radical Jews go to the extent of blocking streets in their quarters on Saturdays to stop cars from passing by and violating religious rules.

The Jewish feasts are the Jewish New Year, the Day of Atonement, Sukkot, Hanukkah (the Jewish Festival of Lights), Purim, and Passover. Arabs, both Muslim and Christian, rarely took part in the Jewish feasts partly because they grew to resent mass Jewish immigration to Palestine, but also because Jews did not encourage non-Jews to share their feasts. The following is a short description of these feasts. The Jewish Calendar is a lunar calendar with intercalated months, so the dates of the festivals change.

Rosh Hashanah
The Jewish New Year, celebrated in September or October, is considered a most important holiday. In the Mishnah, it states that this is the

day when God started creating the world. Traditionally, in the afternoon of this day, Jews go to a river or any flowing water where they pray and have their sins of the past year carried away by the water.

Yom Kippur

The Day of Atonement, in September or October, is one of the most important Jewish feasts. The holiday starts before sunset on the evening prior and continues for about twenty five hours, until after sunset of the next day. This is an important and solemn Jewish holiday, during which Jews fast, attend services, and pray.

Sukkot

The Feast of Tabernacles, celebrated in September or October, lasts for seven days and commemorates the tents of palm leaves that gave shelter to the people of Israel during the 40-year period that they wandered in the wilderness. This day reminds them of the Diaspora. The tradition in this feast is to erect and stay in huts made of branches and leaves, called *Sukkah*, where people pray for rainfall after the dry summer, and celebrate the end of the incoming harvest. In today's modern culture, those who cannot build a *Sukkah* often erect a small parasol on the balcony.

Hanukkah

The Jewish festival of lights (*al-Anwar*), lasts for eight days starting on 25 Kishev (in December). This feast, celebrated around the same time as Christmas, commemorates the rededication of the Holy Temple in Jerusalem, after its destruction in the 2nd century. During this celebration, thousands ascend the hill of Masada.

Purim

Purim, or the Feast of Esther, is celebrated on 14 Adar (in February or March). On this day, Jews have a celebratory meal, drink wine, and perform masquerades. Arabs have given this holiday the name of *'Eid al-Masakhir* (Feast of Masquerade).

Passover

Passover is the feast commemorating the freeing of Jewish slaves from Egypt. According to Jewish tradition, God instructed the Jews to mark the doors of their home with the blood of a lamb, so that their homes would be "passed over" during the tenth plague, which killed all firstborns. Today Passover is a festival of pilgrimage. Keeping Passover requires many complicated rituals, the most important being the avoidance of all leavened foods. Starting the evening before, every Jew makes sure there is no baker's yeast in the house. During Passover, Jews eat unleavened bread baked without yeast or salt. This is in memory of the time when ancient Jews fled Egypt and had no time to allow their bread to rise. Whoever eats bread with yeast on Passover is considered an infidel. In addition to eating matzoh, they must eat bitter herbs. The head of the family relates the story of exodus to which everyone must listen. It is forbidden for Jews to work on the first and the last days of this feast.

PART THREE

Baraziq seller during Ramadan

8.
Play, Pleasure, and Love

SONS AND DAUGHTERS ARE THE JOY OF LIFE in all stages of their life. Grandchildren are an even greater joy. Naturally, families try to instill the traditions of their society in their children. Unconscious imitation is the best way of imparting customs and habits. When older people observe the traditions of their society, children will unconsciously imitate their parents and the people around them and thus absorb the traditions. Dr. Tawfiq Kanaan, in his work on Palestinian folklore, has found a strong relationship between contemporary traditions in Palestine and ancient traditions in the region that have passed from one generation to the next over thousands of years.

Like everywhere in the world, Palestinian children love to play. Modern psychologists have found that playing is an essential activity for children's growth and for developing a well-balanced personality. Contrary to what some parents used to think, it is neither a waste of time nor a useless kind of luxury. Children, therefore, must be encouraged to play. It is unfortunate for society when children of poor parents are forced to work, or when they play on their own, away from the direct supervision of their parents.

Today a great number of toys are manufactured for children, but in the first part of the 20th century and certainly before, children in Palestine had to make their own toys, usually with the help of their parents. Making toys at home out of materials at hand was cheaper and more available. A doll, for example, was made of a piece of cloth, with the shape of a baby drawn on it, then cut and sewn according to the shape drawn and stuffed with torn pieces of cloth. The simple toys of the past enhanced the imaginations and manual skills of children. Such toys were derived from the local environment of the child, therefore conformed to the local culture. It is true that children must be exposed to cultures of other nations, but it is more important for them to be exposed to their own culture.

Children used to play games that varied according to age and gender. Girls of the old days, for example, used to make *Bayt wa duyuf* (house and guests), where a table was made from an empty cigarette packet and chairs from empty match boxes. They would spend time imagining themselves receiving guests, talking to them and offering them coffee and tea, precisely the way their mothers did. Another game for girls was called *hajale* (hopping or hopscotch), where a rectangle with six squares inside it is drawn with chalk on the ground. The playing girl, with one foot on the ground and the other lifted, would try to push a small tile from one square to the other until the tile was pushed out of the rectangle. If her lifted leg touched the ground, or she pushed the tile to the outside before reaching the last square, she lost and gave the turn to the other girl. If she won, she took a square for herself that her partner could not pass through, making it more difficult for the partner to play. Another game was skipping rope, either by one girl alone, or with two holding the ends of the rope. Mothers usually directed their daughters to learn embroidery and knitting, as well as cooking and housekeeping in general.

In the Old City houses, no playgrounds were available for children, so parents installed basic swings for the smaller children, either hung from a tree, the ceiling, or from two windows inside the house. Older children would swing dangerously on them.

There were all kinds of children's songs for almost every game and season. The tunes of these songs remain the same, but words change from time to time or from town to town. Children's songs often reflected the political or social priorities of society at the time. For instance, during the uprising against the British and opposition to Zionist immigration, children's songs reflected the political environment in the country and the whole region. One of these songs goes like this:

> Palestine is my country
> Land of my forefathers
> There I am O Palestine
> Land of glory and faith

Boys played games that were more violent than those of girls. As the people of Palestine were in continuous resistance from the time of the First World War, this was reflected in the games that boys played, as they liked to pretend to be *mujahidin* (resistance fighters). Boys used to make wooden rifles carried on the shoulder with a strap, forming their own military parade in the alleys of their quarter. Their songs again expressed their eagerness to fight the enemy the way grownups did.

There were other games that both boys and girls played, though not together. Catch, known as *zaqquta*, and hide and seek, known as *ghummaidha* (hiding), were both popular. Another game was *hamibared* (hot-cold) where the child had to find something hidden by the group, who call out "hot" or "cold" as he or she gets closer or further away from the hiding place. Another game called *ya 'ammi fain-el-tariq?* (uncle, where is the road?) consists of one child blindfolded trying to catch one of the others by calling out: "Where is the road?"

Another game was called *awwalak ya iskandarani* (you're first, Alexander), a name that indicates nothing of the nature of the game, which is like Leap Frog. A few boys of the same age and size would stand in a row, each about two meters from the other. They all bend over, then the last one jumped over all those in front of him, and this would repeat until everybody has jumped over everybody else. Those who were unable to jump had to leave the game. To make it more difficult, the boys would raise their backs higher. Another version of this game was that the whole group would choose one of them who would bend down and the rest would jump over him, being careful not to dislodge a handkerchief on his back. Anyone who dislodged it had to take the place of the boy bending down. Boys sometimes would cheat by continuing to jump over their friend without confessing that the handkerchief had fallen, until he discovered their cheating. He may then take it with a laugh, or have a quarrel with his friends.

Before sports clubs were established, boys also used to play football in side streets and neighborhoods. Their so-called football was hand-made from old pieces of cloth. Sometimes, if the whole group could collect the money for a ready-made football, they would buy one to play with.

Another boys' game was hopping on one leg, while either running to a goal at a short distance, or with two boys pushing each other until one of them fell and lost.

There was a very interesting toy that we used to play with in our childhood, a *bulbul*, or spinning top. It was a cone-like piece of wood with a small, nail-like metal head at its small end. A thick thread was wound around it with its end tied to the finger of the person using it. When it was thrown skillfully on the ground, it spun on its nail-like end. For a tournament, children would draw a circle and each one had to throw his *bulbul* inside the circle. The winner would be the one whose *bulbul* had spun inside the circle for the longest time. Another way to play was that one player threw his *bulbul* on the ground and the other threw his *bulbul* in such a way that it would hit the first player's *bulbul* and stop its spinning while still spinning on the ground itself.

An interesting hand-made toy for boys was the *al-shu'bah* (twig catapult or slingshot), for hunting birds. This was made from a small piece of wood in the shape of the letter Y, with a piece of strong elastic attached to the two ends, and at the middle of the elastic piece a rectangular piece of leather was attached. A small stone was placed in the piece of leather. The elastic was pulled back and released, strongly shooting the stone out in order to hit a bird and kill it. During the 1987 and 2000 intifadas against the Israeli occupation, Palestinian youngsters widely and effectively used this catapult against the Israeli soldiers. In the past, boys used their catapults in the green hills outside of the town where families would go for entertainment, especially in spring and summer. After the occupation, such outings were stopped.

Another hand-made, and therefore cheap, toy was the hoop, called *dahadil*. A wheel, taken from the cover of a barrel or the inside wiring support of a bicycle tire, was used. Then a thick wire was shaped like the letter Y, with the lower part about one and a half feet (half a meter) long. The wheel was rolled on the ground pushed by the Y-shaped wire. A child either played with it alone, or organized competitions with friends.

Among the pleasurable toys for children forbidden now by the occupation authorities were paper kites. Some young people were real artists at making them. On occasion, prizes were given for the most beautiful kite or for the kite that flew highest. Kites were usually made from bamboo or thin palm wood and paper. They were an excellent source of enjoyment and good brain activators. In addition, they cost almost nothing.

Another toy, even simpler and easier to make was what we called *qubu'*, a paper airplane, which was thrown by hand.

Today children no longer make their own toys. Kites, as well as small cars, can be bought ready-made from the market and flown or moved by batteries or remote control. In addition, the occupation authorities have strictly forbidden all kinds of kites, cutting off enjoyment for the old and young alike.

Daqqa wa Ijri (Hit and Run) was an enjoyable game for older boys. A piece of wood, about four inches (10 centimeters) long, with both ends sharpened was used. The player had to keep hitting the piece of wood on one of the sharp ends with a rough wooden bat. The player lost when it fell on the ground. This game was considered too rough for girls to play.

Playing with marbles was also popular among young boys. A small hole would be dug in the ground and each player would try to hit his playmate's marble and move it to the hole. The winner took a marble from the loser.

In the winter, when the weather was rainy and cold, people played indoor games, like chess and backgammon for men, and *barjis* for women. There was a game that almost all members of the family shared, called *'arusti* (my bride). One of the people playing would be chosen to go out of the room and the rest of the group would agree on an object for that person to guess. After being called in, he or she would ask: "*arusti?*" The group would give him one description of the object and the player kept asking questions until the object was guessed.

Another indoors game for children was what we used to call *tar al-hamam* (the pigeons have flown). When the leader mentions a bird, everyone must raise their hand; if the leader mentions a non-flying animal, they must all keep their hands down. If you made a mistake you were out and the last person in was the winner.

The ring game was also popular. One child would have to guess which child had a ring hidden in their hand. Each child would try to pretend to have the ring by enlarging his closed hands or by other ploys. The child whose turn it was might try to guess by looking at the other children's faces.

In the tray-and-cups game, three or four cups were placed on a tray and something was placed under one of the cups. A child had to discover the hidden object, and otherwise had to pay a price, like singing or dancing or whatever the player who had hidden the object demanded.

Riddles were also very popular. Many belonged to old Arab traditions and were written in poetic form or with rhymed phrases. That is why they are difficult to translate to other languages. Examples are the following:

> What's a naked one that dresses all people? (a needle)
> What's fluffy hair that's neither cotton nor wool? (snow)
> What's a bowl that dives in the sea, inside of which are pearls and the outside is copper? (a pomegranate)
> What's a red city, with green walls, black inhabitants, having an iron key? (a watermelon)
> What's something that has a bottom of water and a head of fire? (a *nargile*, hubble-bubble)
> What's something that becomes large when you take from it and small when you add into it? (a ditch)

III

It may be that children of old times were cleverer in such games than present-day children who, unfortunately, receive their games and toys ready-made.

In winter evenings particularly, grandmothers were greatly sought after by children for their ability to relate fabulous stories and anecdotes that were mostly taken from traditional works, such as *Alf Laylah wa Laylah*, known in the West as the *Arabian Nights*. The custom of listening to tales told by grandmothers stimulated children's imagination. In addition, the whole family used to gather together listening to the grandmother's tales, instilling a feeling of social warmth in the children's subconscious, as compared with present day television programs and computer games that keep family members either silent or playing alone. Tales told by grandmothers had a special protocol with the idea of exciting listeners before the tale started. In these narratives, supernatural creatures were the main characters of the tales. The ghoul in these tales stands up as the most popular, albeit fearful, character. Sometimes coming as male, and sometimes as female (*ghoula* or *'amurah*), the ghoul is able to perform supernatural actions, like carrying a human being to fabulously distant and strange places, traveling through time, past or future, to meet historical people or people who have not been born, or committing supernaturally savage actions. *Jinns* (genies) and *afarit* (pl. of *ifrit*) are also supernatural creatures, and confusion between the three is quite common. Some of these creatures are good and friendly with humans, while some others are bad and hurtful. In short, they represent human nature in an exaggerated manner.

Children's songs have always expressed either the social situation of the people or the major events that effected people's lives in Palestine. One of the songs that both children and adults used to sing was one that went around after Sheikh Izzeddin al-Qassam was martyred in combat with the British army on 19 November 1935 during a Palestinian uprising.

> Izzeddin whom we lost
> You've been martyred for your people

> How we wish you were still alive
> You, leader of the Mujahidin!

As the British failed to curb the 1936 uprising in Palestine, an important officer by the name of General Dill was dispatched to take over. The following song, by the popular poet and singer Nuh Ibrahim, gained great popularity:

> Take care, Mr. Dill
> It may be solved by your good hands
> But don't think the nation will lose hope
> If you think you can solve it by force
> You must know for sure
> That your goal is impossible
> You better be wise
> And heed the nation's demands
> Liberty and independence
> Take care, Mr. Dill

Another one came to be when Allen Sikrist, the British Police Commissioner in Jerusalem, was assassinated by two young Arab revolutionaries in 1936. The song was expressive of people's happiness about the news, as he had been known for his savage and rude behavior towards the Palestinian people. Two lines of the song are:

> Sikrist dead, Sikrist dead
> Seven bullets in his head!

During the 1936 revolution, children used to imitate revolutionaries by carrying mock rifles made of wood on their shoulders, marching like soldiers, and singing their expressive songs, like:

> O, Zionist, run away
> The revolutionaries have shown up
> Led by Fawzi Qawuqji
> The hero of the intrepid battalion

Another song goes like this:

> Father has brought me a gift
> A machine gun and a rifle
> Tomorrow when I'm grown-up
> I'll join the liberation army

After 1967, children's songs changed words. An example is the following:

> Taq, taq, taqiyya
> America is the snake's head
> We want a state and an identity
> In the West Bank and Gaza
> Which we'll achieve
> By our people's revolt!
> Victorious we are, victorious we are
> Against America and Israel
> I'm a small Arab child
> I fight with the commandos
> I'm three years old
> But my heart is strong like granite
> Zionists in front of me are weak
> Suffice it that I'm an Arab

There are other children's songs that were sung for fun on various occasions. A famous one that was sung during cold rainy winters goes like this:

> Rain, rain, lots of rain
> Our house is built with iron
> Uncle Abdallah has broken the jar
> And grandfather said to him
> Go out, go out!

Another funny song goes like this:

> Fly, pigeon, fly
> And go to my grandfather
> But grandfather is in Mecca
> He gave me a cake
> Which I've hidden in a box
> But the box has no key
> And the key is with the blacksmith
> The blacksmith wants money
> And money is with the sultan
> The sultan has a baby boy
> The baby needs milk
> But the milk is with the goat
> And the goat needs weeds

And the weeds need water
Water is at the will of God
No God but He
Muhammad is his messenger!

Christian children also had their special songs. Here's one:

I've laid my head on my cot
With seven crosses over my head
As I mentioned the name of Jesus
All his bibles were opened
Three saints appeared
Peter, Paul, and John the Baptist
Who take care of us day and night!

In addition to these songs, the words of which were in Palestinian Arabic, pupils at school used to learn national hymns or anthems written by well-known Arab contemporary poets. These hymns were very popular and are still sung today. One of the most famous anthems was *Mawtini* (My Homeland), by Ibrahim Tuqan, which is still chanted today on national occasions, not only by Palestinians but by all Arabs.

Ever since the first intifada in 1987, the life of Palestinian children has radically changed. The uprising was a clear expression of the Palestinians' feeling of despair toward a seemingly endless Israeli occupation of the Palestinian territories. The occupation has been characterized by daily arrests of men and women; torturing of prisoners; confiscation of land; and destruction of agricultural land, particularly the uprooting of olive trees, which are a traditionally sacred—and an important source of income—for the Palestinians throughout history. All this had the objective of forcing people to leave their homeland so that it would be possible for Jewish immigrants to establish a purely Jewish state in Palestine. The 1987 intifada was called *intifadat al-hijara* (the uprising of stones), for it was mainly Palestinian youngsters who, in a mass uprising throughout the country, started attacking the heavily armed Israeli soldiers with stones, the only weapon they had in hand. The savage reaction of the Israelis not only deprived Palestinian children of the natural joy of youth but also brought about deep psychological repercussions for Israeli soldiers who found themselves like Goliath facing David. Once again, songs whose words came from the situation were on everybody's tongue. Another effect the intifada had on Palestinian youth was that they started using their traditional games for real action as intifada tools, namely the stone and its shooting *nuqqaifa* and *muqlai'a* (catapult). In their free time after school, boys trained in their play, aiming stones at their own targets. For Palestinian children, boys and girls, watching the news became more important than watching children's TV shows, and they began inquiring about the history of the Arab-Zionist struggle from their parents and teachers. Even children's dreams for the future were affected by the incidents. Some children began to dream of establishing a factory for manufacturing explosives to fight the Jews. Children and young people who witnessed Palestinians being killed in encounters with the heavily armed Israeli army and were told that these martyrs would be taken to Heaven, became more faithful and keen on observing prayers. At the same time, with the constant shooting by Israeli soldiers and the savage bombardment of Arab towns and villages by Israeli airplanes and helicopters, small Palestinian children were scared and suffered from the psychological consequences of this condition. To a few of them, such atrocities became commonplace and apparently caused little fear. Those children who could get hold of empty bullets and bombs used them for playing. In addition, many children were killed as a result of random shooting by Israeli soldiers; some cases caught by television cameras showed that shooting at children was intentional and not a result of being caught in crossfire.[14]

Going out to the mountains and valleys, especially in spring and summer, had been a popular habit in the whole country before the Israeli occupation. While on these outings, people enjoyed eating many kinds of natural flora that grew in the mountains and valleys, other plants were avoided because of their harmful effects on the skin. Children also used to collect healthy herbs, like sage and chamomile, which grew naturally in the mountains and valleys. Those outings were seasonal and had nothing to do with religious occasions. A place called *Sa'ad & Sa'id*, in the suburbs of Jerusalem, was quite popular among the families of Jerusalem. Going out, people used to take food and drink with them and enjoy the beautiful nature of the Palestinian countryside. Today, with the Israeli occupation, Palestinians have almost no place to go to for any outing. This has caused many psychological problems among young people, driving them to violence, sometimes against each other.

Tamer Hindi (sweet soft drink) seller on the streets of Jerusalem

9.
Evenings of Pleasure

JERUSALEM IS KNOWN FOR BEING THE HOME of Christian and Muslim sacred sanctuaries, like the Church of the Holy Sepulchre, al-Aqsa Mosque, and the Dome of the Rock. Jerusalem has also been known for its theological schools and high-ranking theologians of both religions. However, the people of Jerusalem have also enjoyed the various arts of music, singing, and folk dancing.

The people of Jerusalem, like the rest of Greater Syria, suffered a lot from the oppression imposed by the Ottomans, followed by the British. The rule of the British in Palestine led to a continuous revolution against their occupation and particularly against the Jewish immigration that was encouraged and strongly supported by the British.

Despite all of this, the people of Jerusalem have never lost their blithe spirit and have enjoyed their various festivals on every occasion. Others, sarcastically perhaps, accuse the people of Jerusalem of being too serious, a characteristic that has many bizarre explanations. However, the fact remains that the people of Jerusalem are a homogeneous group. Unlike the seaports of Jaffa and Haifa, where people were constantly receiving visitors from various countries of the world, Jerusalem had more of a closed society. Jaffa, in particular, with its cafés, entertainment places, and artists coming from many places, was considered the city of arts in Palestine. Jerusalem's celebrations of popular festivals were different from celebrations in the villages and some other towns in Palestine. Group dancing and singing that were common in the villages, like *dabka* and traditional singing, were not popular in Jerusalem. Due to the conservative nature of Jerusalemites and others, such as the people of Hebron and Nablus, men and women did not mix together for parties and celebrations. However, in their own celebrations, women enjoyed full freedom to sing and dance. At the beginning of the 20th century, many musical festivals were celebrated, some of which were attended by the famous Lebanese singer, Badi'a Masabni. For wedding parties, a team of Aleppo Jews, called Dallaniyya, used to play old Andalusian Arab music and songs, called *muwashshahat*.

In 1910, the phonograph was introduced into the city for the first time and was sold for 25 French francs, a price that only rich people could afford. A few cafés, however, were keen enough to have it as a way of attracting customers. Listening to recorded songs of the then famous singers, like Sheikh Minyalawi, Salameh Hijazi, Sayyed Darwish, Munira al-Mahdiyya, and Badi'a Masabni was quite a breakthrough in technology. I remember how funny it was when the song started to fade away, indicating that the phonograph needed to be wound up again, by turning its handle clockwise. There were also petty quarrels that took place at popular cafés between customers when each one insisted on his favorite song or singer. The typical café stools at that time were square, with wooden legs 15–20 inches (40–50 centimeters) high, with a woven straw seat and no backrest. At the entrance to the café was a kitchenette where coffee, tea, and other hot drinks were prepared. In summer, cooled beverages, like lemonade and fizzy drinks, were served. Cold drinks were cooled by pieces of ice procured from ice-making factories. The *nargile* was also a major service offered to café customers. In the evenings, cafés were lit with oil lanterns, but normally, outside the month of Ramadan, they were closed down soon after sunset.

There were a number of reasons for café customers to return home early in the evening. One was due to security, a reason used by both the Ottoman and the British authorities, for they did not want people to gather together lest they plot against the authorities. Another reason was the fact that alleys were not lit and the gates of the Old City were locked at night to prevent thieves from entering the city. The fact that the city lanes and narrow alleys were not lit made people afraid of the 'amurah. This fabulous creature was thought to be a daughter of *jinns* or a female *ghoul* and seems to be a relatively modern invention, as it was not mentioned in the old traditional tales. The 'amurah was said to be a black, tall, and broad creature that blocked lanes and prevented anyone who encountered it from passing unless he carried it on his back. But then, the 'amurah would stick its feet to the ground so that the man carrying it could not move. A few people claimed to have been attacked by this creature, but such a story was never heard from two people walking together. Whatever it was, the panic caused by this creature in Jerusalem society served homemakers well, as they wanted their men to come home at an early hour. It was also useful to the authorities, who did not want gatherings of men in the evenings.

Cafés in Jerusalem were attended by men only, mostly from outside the city, as quite a few people of Jerusalem abstained from sitting in cafés. In fact, one of the questions asked about the behavior of a young man proposing to a girl was whether he had been regularly attending cafés. For a certain class of people, cafés were considered places for wasting time, perhaps gambling and drinking alcohol. The last two habits were taboo in respectable Jerusalem society. There was a café owner in 1918 by the name of Khalil Jawhariyya, who gained certain serving skills from Beirut, like offering a meal of *mezze* with *arak*, the local alcoholic drink. His café became an attraction for music lovers, as he was famous for inviting the best Arab singers to sing at his café. Badi'a Masabni and her husband, Najib Rayhani, were two celebrities in the world of art who were among his famous guests. His brother, Wassef, was a famous professional lute player who performed his art at that café, as well as at the houses of certain Jerusalem notables who kept girlfriends in palaces outside the Old City walls.

During the evenings of Ramadan, cafés attracted a large clientele by hosting singers who specialized in the traditional songs praising of Prophet Muhammad. Another popular activity was having storytellers, called *ruwat* or *hakawatis*, tell the old Arab epics, like *Abu Zayd al-Hilali*,

Sayf ibn Dhi Yazan, and *'Antara*. The *hakawati* was a gifted man who could remember by heart an epic that he told in a lively, dramatic way. According to what was happening in the narrative, he skillfully played with his voice and waved with his arm or stick. Sometimes, people in the audience would react excitedly, protesting tempestuously when their fictional hero was defeated for a while or taken prisoner by a formidable enemy. The *hakawati* recited long epics that took a few evenings to tell, and used crucial stopping points to leave his audience suspended and eager for the next evening. Some people would reject the crisis of the hero and argue with the *hakawati*, who would eventually acquiesce and promise to release the hero the next evening. Sometimes, some of the audience would support one hero, while another group supported another hero. Such a situation would naturally give rise to petty skirmishes among the audience. If this happened, the *hakawati* took care to calm down the audience.

Storytelling had a special protocol. The *hakawati* put on his best clothes, and covered his head with an *'imama*, *kufiyya* (checked cloth), or *tarbush* (fez). He sat on an elevated podium in a corner of the café, where everybody was able to see him and he was able to see all his audience and notice their reaction. He started with saluting the audience, requesting God to bless the Prophet Muhammad, as well as all the prophets of God. Then he gave a long prologue before starting his tale or epic. It is important to note that storytelling was so respected that no sound would be heard when the *hakawati* spoke.

As a natural result of the appearance of modern means of entertainment, the demand for *hakawatis* decreased, and they stopped their recitations completely after the 1967 occupation. However, such epics encouraged heroism against enemies. The epic of *al-Dhaher Baybar*, which praised the Egyptian king of that name who defeated the Crusaders and expelled them from Jerusalem and the whole region, was particularly relevant to the ongoing occupation. As a result, the Israeli occupying authorities could not tolerate such an art form.

Another form of entertainment at the cafés was puppet theater, which was, in its criticism of the rulers and the political and social scene, similar to the present-day political cartoons in newspapers. As this theater used to address people of different standards of living and education, it changed its topics according to its audience.

In the new city of Jerusalem, immigrant Jews had their cafés too. In addition to serving alcohol, they offered a new kind of attraction that was unusual for the conservative Arab society of Jerusalem: girls serving customers while wearing seductive European dress. Some young Arabs had intimate relations with these girls, sometimes for fun, but sometimes, against the will of their relatives, their relations ended with marriage. Many of these marriages failed, but a few were successful and some Jewish wives willingly converted to Islam. I personally remember a Jewish neighbor who became a very faithful Muslim, followed Muslim traditional customs, and maintained excellent relationships with all her Arab neighbors. Quite a few of these couples had children who, when adults, joined the uprising and fought the Zionist immigrants side by side with their Arab brothers. After the 1967 Israeli occupation of Jerusalem, children born to Jewish mothers and Muslim fathers were offered special treatment if they "went back" to Judaism, on the grounds that children of Jewish women were considered Jews by birth. However, they often invariably refused.

After the 1948 occupation of the western part of Jerusalem, cafés in the Old City remained as they were, but new cafés appeared in the new quarters outside the Old City wall. After the 1967 Israeli occupation, cafés were semi-deserted as they became preferred places for the agents of the Israeli intelligence, called *musta'ribin*. They were so named because they pretended to be Arabs, speaking fluent Arabic and dressing like Arabs. Their task was to spy on what people said at the cafés and to arrest Arabs participating in the Resistance. Those cafés later became places for drug addicts and Israeli prostitutes. In the Old City, many new cafés and restaurants were opened, but, unfortunately, lacked the traditional indigenous atmosphere.

In the 1930s, the theater started to compete with the cafés in offering entertainment, when a few of the most famous Egyptian drama teams, like that of Yusuf Wahbi, started showing their plays in Jerusalem. Local theater troops from Jaffa also used to come present their plays in Jerusalem.

Schools had their own drama activities and they usually had their big performances at the end of the academic year. Drama activities were also held by the various clubs and societies, as well as the Palestinian Broadcasting Service (*Huna'l-Quds*). The latter was a radio station that started in the mid-1930s, broadcasting for a few hours in its early days. Most of the time it was in Arabic, but there was a program in English and another in Hebrew. At the beginning, the number of listeners was small but gradually increased. The radio used to broadcast old and famous songs, but the news was the foremost attraction for people. However, because the news came from official sources, it did not satisfy people's thirst for information, especially in times of turmoil. The first director of the broadcasting service was the Palestinian poet, Ibrahim Tuqan, who was later replaced by 'Ajaj Nuweihed. The most famous local singers were Yusuf Ridhwan, Khalil Salman, and Fahd al-Najjar. It was Nizar Abu'l-Su'ud who read the last news bulletin for the Palestinian Broadcasting Service (*Huna'l-Quds*) on the night of May 15, 1948, just before the end of the British Mandate and the closing down of this service. The only broadcasting service left in Jerusalem after that date was that of *al-Jihad al-Muqaddas* (*the holy jihad*), which used to broadcast from a station powered by a battery. The man who did the broadcasting was killed while on duty. The Near East Arabic Broadcasting Service (*al-Sharq al-Adna*) in Jaffa was a strong rival to *Huna'l-Quds*. This broadcasting service was established as a propaganda tool for the Allies in the Second World War. After 1947 it was transferred to Cyprus.

Talking about folk songs, it must be mentioned that almost all these songs used to praise the land and its produce, emotionally combining such praise with praise of a beloved sweetheart. These folk songs were popular in most Arab countries, particularly in Greater Syria and Iraq, with changes in words from one village to another, sometimes according to the occasion. Usually, a folk song is started by a *muwwal*, a vocal improvisation or prelude, which has its origins in ancient Arab history, and commenced with a melancholic tune, expressing either a sad event or the sad fact that a beloved is far away. After the Palestinian Nakba of 1948, these songs remained popular, but referred to the homeland as the beloved one, sometimes by changing words, but many times by allusion. Many Palestinians cannot help but shed tears when they listen to these songs.

In Jerusalem, as well as in a few other Palestinian towns, women had what was called an *istiqbal* (reception) day. Almost every married woman had a specific day of the month on which she would receive her women friends. Such receptions were occasions for women to see each other, chat, sing and dance, and play *barjis*, their preferred game. Preparations for this day would start a few days earlier, when the house would be meticulously cleaned. Coffee, tea, and soft drinks, as well as tobacco for *nargiles* for those who smoked, were made available to visitors. Some sweets and light food, according to the financial position of the receiving woman, would also be prepared to be offered to the guests. Except for older girls, children were not allowed to sit with the women and sometimes they are sent to stay with relatives until the end of the reception. Receptions started in the afternoon and continued until sunset, unless there was a special occasion that justified staying later in the evening. When political turmoil takes place, women's conversation and singing reflect the general conditions in the country.

Al-Mawlid means the birthday of Prophet Muhammad. *Al-Mawlid* parties, in spite of the connotation of the word, had no special time, as they were always a welcome activity because of the traditional songs that praised the Prophet. People used to set up such parties on certain important occasions, like when a boy was born, a pupil completed school, or a prisoner was released. At such parties, singing songs in praise of the Prophet by specialized men or women has always been considered a blessing or a kind of worship. Such parties may continue until late at night, when the women would be picked up by their men. Women singers would be escorted home by the house owners or might spend the night at the house.

Nabi Musa procession

10.
Festivals and Popular Occasions

MEN AND WOMEN, OLD AND YOUNG, everybody shared in the parties and festivals that bonded the people and acted as an expression of national unity.

Dr Kamal al-Asali, in his book, *The Nabi Musa Festival in Palestine*, emphasizes the fact that popular festivals are related to the various seasons of the year. Originally, before the appearance of Islam, they were based on Christian feasts, which in turn were a continuation of the festivals worshipping the old gods. Examples are feasts that were celebrated in springtime and expressed in slaying animals as sacrifices to the gods, as well as coloring the hands with henna, and coloring animals red. Such festivals, throughout history, expressed social and economic needs. They also kept members of Palestinian society close to each other, and provided the individual with a feeling of belonging, giving people the necessary energy to work and produce. Eating and drinking, singing and dancing, as well as other means of entertainment, have always accompanied celebrations and festivals. Many of them followed a period of fasting. It is important to mention here that agricultural produce played an important part in these festivals. That is why springtime, expressing life's renewal, was a strong motive for many kinds of festivals.

The protocols of festivals have been copied from one nation or religion by another. When a new religion prevails, it adopts, with necessary adaptations, many of the rituals of the old religion. International Labor Day on May 1, to cite an example, goes back to the celebration of fertility in springtime. Christmas goes back to an old midwinter festival celebrated by the Romans between December 17 and 24, as well as to a similar Persian festival.

This is the context for the annual festivals celebrated by Palestinians. In springtime, we have festivals for al-Nabi Musa (the Prophet Moses), al-Nabi Salih, al-Husain ibn 'Ali, and Wadi al-Naml. In summertime, the harvest time for the Canaanites, the al-Nabi Rubin festival is celebrated.

After the liberation of Jerusalem from the Crusaders on October 2, 1187, Salah ad-Din (Saladin), following the steps of 'Umar ibn al-Khattab, delivered the keys of the Church of the Holy Sepulchre to the two old Jerusalem families: Joudeh and Nusseibeh, as mentioned earlier. Salah ad-Din, in addition to having a group of Muslims carefully watch foreigners visiting the Church of the Holy Sepulchre, introduced a few Islamic festivals that were, in most cases, in line with the old timings of Christian festivals. The purpose of these festivals was to gather Muslims together as a protection against any possible attack from the Crusaders.

The first and most important of these festivals was al-Nabi Musa, held at a place located about 15 miles (25 kilometers) away from Jerusalem, at a strategic point on the route to the citadel of Karak, east of the Dead Sea, which was still occupied by the Crusaders. Saladin wanted Muslims to gather fully armed in that place, where a shrine was built for that purpose, at a time of the year when Christians were celebrating Easter at the Church of the Holy Sepulchre. The shrine gradually became a sacred place visited by pilgrims from the various Islamic countries, as they came from Mecca to Jerusalem to complete their pilgrimage. In time, people started to weave stories around this place with its black rocks and occasional strong winds that would collapse visitors' tents. These natural phenomena were interpreted as the result of people committing certain sins in the place, such as allowing a menstruating woman to enter.

Preparations for this festival were of great importance in all major cities, like Nablus and al-Khalil (Hebron), together with their surrounding villages. Participants would wear new and beautiful clothes, merchants would take advantage of the occasion to sell their merchandise, artists would prepare their drama groups to present shows at the place, and particularly Sufis would be ready to perform their rituals. As its date coincides with Easter, in accordance with the Greek Orthodox Church, which is related to the appearance of the full moon, it occurs in April or early May each year. It starts on the Friday that precedes the Orthodox Christian Good Friday and continues till the following Thursday. This Friday is called *Jum'at al-Nazla* (the Descending Friday). Other celebrations and preparations start before this time, the most important being *Jum'at al-Munadah* (the Calling Friday). This comes one week before *Jum'at al-Nazla*, and is meant to officially announce the onset of the festival in the coming week. The city notables and high-ranking officials would attend court and witness the official announcement of the festival. This *Munadah* (calling) used to take place at the old building of the Shari'a Court at al-Silsila Gate. In 1967, the court building was occupied by the Israeli army and used as a security center; later it was turned into a Talmudic school. The Thursday night before *Jum'at al-Nazla* is called *Laylat al-Waq'a*, when people who intended to participate in the festival prepared themselves for the forthcoming days and friends and families coordinated with each other. Traditionally, each major clan had its own *bayraq* (flag), which was kept at a special place called *Dar al-Bayraq* (Flag House). The flags that belonged to the Sufis were kept at their *zawaya*. The most famous Sufi *bayraq* was the one called *Bayraq al-Dissi*, named after Sheikh 'Atif al-Dissi, who, when young, was a first class drummer, and later became leader of the Sufi parade.

The Nabi Musa parade started on Friday morning when the main *bayraq* was brought from *Dar al-Bayraq*, located at the western side of al-Aqsa Mosque. It was then presented to the Mufti, who, after reading *al-Fatiha* (the first *sura* of the Holy Qur'an), unfolded the flag and tied it to the pole. The procession moved slowly toward the mosque, entering from the gate at *Bab al-Majlis*. After Friday prayers, the parade started its march, with all the Jerusalem notables in the front line. The procession was accompanied by a team of drummers, called *sayyara*, whose members belonged to certain Jerusalem clans who inherited this honor from their forefathers. Carriers of the flags marched in front of the procession. In fact, the flag carriers are carried on the shoulders of several enthusiastic men who chanted at the top of their voices: *Ya halali wa ya mali*, which is repeated by the participants in the parade. Then the procession marched out through *Bab Hutta*, where a greater crowd was gathered. When the parade reached *Bab al-Asbat* (Lion's Gate), the Mufti mounted a white horse, as did the rest of the notables who proceeded on horseback toward the *Jithmaniyya* road carrying their flags. The crowds on both sides of the street saluted the parade, chanting popular songs and spraying rose water. The crowds would be so huge that for one to secure a place in front to watch the parade one had to arrive very early in the morning. When the procession reached *Ras al-'Amud*, it was honorably received by the city mayor and council at a large tent that was specially built for the occasion. After that, it continued its march to the Nabi Musa Sanctuary. After the procession left the city, people went back to al-Aqsa Mosque, gathering in the courtyard where they carried on their celebration throughout the day. The Nabi Musa Sanctuary is located 15 miles (25 kilometers) to the east of Jerusalem, off the road to Jericho. Nabi Musa is not buried there, but the sanctuary was built in his honor. The same is true of many other similar sanctuaries in the country.

Various delegations from all over the country used to come to Jerusalem to participate in the festival and parade. The most interesting moment, however, would be the meeting of the two delegations from Nablus and al-Khalil (Hebron). A great competition would start between the two groups, each one trying to outdo the other in its dances and songs. *Dabka* used to instigate the hottest competition between these two prominent delegations.

The festival was a good time for merchants to display their merchandise, making use of such a large gathering. Many people made vows to distribute meat among the poor during that sacred occasion, so the occasion was excellent time for merchants of livestock, particularly sheep, to sell their merchandise. In spite of the fact that food was available free of charge to attendants, served inside special rooms at the sanctuary premises, outside the premises were makeshift cafés and restaurants for people who wanted a different fare. In the way of entertainment, children enjoyed their games and the youth enjoyed horseback riding, as well as watching the sword-and-shield games and wrestling matches. *Sanduq al-'ajayeb* (chest of wonders) was like the cinema of today; this large box contained a roll of photographs representing the heroes of ancient Arab epics, like 'Antara and Abu-Zayd al-Hilali. Four or five children would sit on a bench in front the chest, look inside it through small glass windows, and see the photographs enlivened by the chest operator as he moved them while relating the epic in a musical way. Monkeys were also an interesting entertainment, as trained monkeys would mimic people in various displays. In addition to all of this, there were magicians who had very interesting shows, which attracted a great crowd.

Many people had their male babies circumcised at the sanctuary during the festival. The same celebration for circumcision as described before was carried out at the sanctuary, and the "surgeons" were adulated.

This popular gathering at the Nabi Musa sanctuary was also an occasion for political parties to hold meetings and give speeches. Demonstrations of rival parties often came to the verge of bloody fights. However, wise notables were always ready to interfere to keep the demonstrations peaceful.

National hymns expressing the political problems of the country were generally well known, and the Nabi Musa festival was one of the occasions when these hymns were chanted by the crowds. The following are examples:

> O lions of war
> Our enemy has exceeded all limits
> Let's all die
> For the sake of our homeland
>
> Sons of Syria
> Sons of Iraq

Sons of Egypt
Have you forgotten a great era
When we prevailed on all horizons

The land of the Arabs is our homeland
From Damascus to Baghdad
From Najd to Yemen
To Egypt and Tetuan

O darkness of the prison
We do love darkness
For after night
A dawn shall come

On Wednesday evening, the festival came to an end and people prepared to leave the sanctuary. On Thursday morning, the delegations with their flags started their march back to Jerusalem. At the village of Silwan, near Jerusalem, the procession stopped at a large tent built by the people of Silwan to welcome the Mufti and the delegations. Food was served to the whole crowd and *dabka* dancers showed their beautiful art. After the guests had eaten and had some rest, a delegation would arrive from Jerusalem through Wadi 'l-Jawz to invite the parade to Jerusalem. The procession started its march into the holy city, with the players of the sword-and-shield in front. The Mufti marched in front of the parade, with the chanters and carriers of the flags around him, until the crowd reached al-Aqsa Mosque. As the crowd entered the mosque precinct, carriers of the flags would compete to see who could have his flag tied to the highest tree. There, divided into many circles of singers and dancers, the crowds continued singing their popular songs and dancing *dabka*.

On Friday evening, the celebrations came to an end and the delegations from all over the country left the city, carrying their *bayraqs*, in the majestic way they had come in.

After the British occupation of Palestine, the Nabi Musa Festival gained a national and political character. The celebration of 1920 was a starting point in the resistance against the British occupation of Palestine and their encouragement of European Jewish immigration into the country. In this regard, it is important to mention that the Christians started to play a large part in the festival, side by side with the Muslims. On Friday morning, April 2, 1920, delegations from all over the country filled Jerusalem. A great number of Christians carrying their flags were among the crowds who started their march from al-Aqsa Mosque. At Jaffa Gate the British forces tried in vain to stop the crowds, but eventually had to allow them to march on. However, some of the radical Zionists, lead by Vladimir Jabotinsky, exploded a hand grenade in the crowd, which resulted in a clash between the Arabs and the British and European Jews.

Other places in the country had similar festivals, like that of Nabi Salih at Ramla, Darum at Gaza, Mintar and al-Husain at 'Askalan. For the purpose of such festivals, shrines and sanctuaries were built everywhere in the country, but, as mentioned earlier, the names given to them did not necessarily have real historical connections.

Although many of those festivals were stopped after the Israeli occupation of Palestine in 1948, and particularly after 1967, people nowadays try to revive some of these festivals, especially that of al-Nabi Musa. In 1987 and in 1999, a group of Sufis celebrated the occasion, but the traditional marches from the various cities were impossible.

During this period of the year, Jerusalem was crowded with people, both Muslim and Christian, the former celebrating al-Nabi Musa and the latter celebrating Easter.

Officially, Easter celebrations take one week, but people used to extend the celebrations for a longer time. As with the al-Nabi Musa Festival, preparations for Easter began a long time before, with the knowledge that the date of Easter differed from one Christian denomination to another. The most important Easter celebration, that of the Greek Orthodox Church, coincides with al-Nabi Musa.

Easter celebrations officially began on Palm Sunday. The parade started at 'Ayzariyya and moved toward Beit Faja, Jithmaniyya, Bab al-Asbat (Lion's Gate), al-Salahiyya, al-Wad, 'Aqbat al-Saraya, Khan al-Zayt Gate, 'Aqbat al-Khammarat, and the Christian Quarter, until the 14 stages of the Via Dolorosa were covered. In the front of the parade, an archer, called *al-qawwas*, marched carrying a long staff with an ornamented metal head and a thick metal base. Wearing a long dress with a waistcoat ornamented with gold threads, a fez on his head and a sword at his waist, he marched raising the staff up and letting it down in a regular manner, sounding a loud rhythm. His strong physique and majestic dress imparted him with a special aura of awe and respect.

The position of *al-qawwas* was reserved for Muslims from certain Jerusalem clans who inherited this honor generation after generation. Originally, this position started from the time of Caliph 'Umar ibn al-Khattab who had appointed a strong Muslim bodyguard for each Christian patriarch to protect him and open the road during his movements in the city. This custom remained until the time of the Crusaders. When the Crusaders were forced out of Jerusalem, the position of *al-qawwas* was resumed by Salah ad-Din and continued from that time until today. Behind *al-qawwas*, the patriarch marched with his ornamented cloak and embroidered headdress, carrying the patriarchal staff, ornamented with ivory and silver. Around the patriarch were the monks, priests, and other men of the church. Alongside them, in addition to men carrying crosses and large candles, marched men carrying palm branches that were usually woven into the shape of the cross. Musical teams and scouts also shared in the procession. Our grandfathers told us that in the old days patriarchs used to ride on donkeys and wore a crown of thorns on their heads, emulating our master Lord Jesus Christ. I never saw this custom in my lifetime. The procession stopped at the Church of the Holy Sepulchre, where prayers were said.

On Holy Thursday, called "Washing Thursday" in Arabic, the Greek Orthodox Patriarch, as described earlier, commemorates Jesus Christ's washing the feet of his disciples, by washing the feet of 12 priests, with the archdeacon pouring water from a special jug.

11.
Economic Traditions

EVERYWHERE IN THE WORLD, there is a direct relationship between social life and economic conditions. Both have a tangible effect on each other.

Perhaps all of the Abrahamic religions urge work. There are many popular sayings in Arabic that show how people in the past believed in the necessity of an active life and diligent work, for example: "Activity is blessed," "A craft in hand enables one to own the citadel," and "I was a shepherd until my arm raised me!"

With the developments that have accompanied modern life, a few old crafts have disappeared. These crafts were an important part of social traditions in Jerusalem, and it is important to discuss them here.

The city of Jerusalem has a special nature, in the sense that it is actually two cities in one. The ancient city inside the wall has preserved its architectural and social character over many centuries. Starting in the second half of the 19th century, all modern development and change has taken place outside the wall. During this time, since the Old City was unable to cope with the increasing population, rich residents of Jerusalem started building their houses outside the wall in the new quarters of Sheikh Jarrah and Bab al-Sahira to the north and Baq'a to the south. To the west of the Old City, a few Jewish settlements were built. New roads to Jericho, Nablus, and Jaffa were constructed, and in 1892 the vital railway between Jerusalem and Jaffa opened.

In 1905, the alleys and streets of the Old City were lit with gasoline lamps. Early in the 20th century, the houses of the new city were provided with electricity, but the Old City had to wait until the 1930s. The city was provided with piped water in 1918.

The fact that Jerusalem enjoys a sacred status for Muslims, Christians, and Jews meant that it was frequented by pilgrims from all over the world. This situation had a strong effect on the local customs and traditions. For the same reason, Jerusalem has been an important commercial center, linking the northern and southern parts of Greater Syria with each other. It has also been an important junction between the coastal cities and the hinterland. Over the centuries, this gave rise to a class of merchants with a special character. It also gave rise to special industries catering to the needs of tourists. The prevalence of olive trees in the country made olive wood, with its hardness and characteristic texture, an important material for making religious icons and other carvings that were attractive to tourists.

Thanks to its special religious status, Jerusalem has been a learning center and a place for numerous and various religious schools, Islamic and Christian. This led to the rise of a class of people linked to different kinds of educational activity.

The green areas outside the walls of Jerusalem were never enough to provide the city with its needs as regards vegetables, fruit, or meat. Therefore, the city was dependent on neighboring villages for such vital provisions, which made the city a vital place for villagers who traveled into the city each day to sell their produce and buy the needed supplies.

All these factors created cosmopolitan society with diverse habits and traditions.

Water was scarce in Jerusalem, with only a couple of small springs located outside the city, namely Ayyub Well and Silwan Spring. Houses in the past depended on rain water collected into wells during the wintertime. The water would later be bailed out in the traditional way, with a bucket. When manual water pumps appeared, a few houses utilized this novelty. In the streets, there were *sabils* (public fountains) that provided tourists and passers-by with free water.

In summertime, rainwater wells were not always sufficient. Water had to be carried to houses in leather skins by a *saqqa'* (water carrier). Those *saqqa's*, who carried water skins on their backs or, if the distance was long, on donkeys, used to bring water from the water wells at al-Aqsa Mosque or at Sabil as-Silsila. People used to pay the *saqqa'* either a fixed amount each month, or according to the number of skins they needed. In the latter case, every time the *saqqa'* brought water, he would make a mark on the front wall of the house, at the end of the week or month he would calculate the number of marks on the wall and receive his payment accordingly. Water carrying was one of the oldest jobs in the society. It was also a tiring and unrewarding work, although a few *saqqa's* were able to make a fortune out of the job. The craft had its rules with a kind of syndicate and an officially elected leader. The syndicate had the purpose of protecting its members and organizing their activities, for instance by allocating the area where each member was supposed to serve. Election of the leader of this craft, as well as other crafts, was officially registered at the *Shari'a* court. In the Old City, water carriers served a need until the 1940s, although the houses of the new city had been provided with running water earlier. After May 15, 1948, as a result of the Israeli occupation of the western part of Jerusalem, water from Ras al-'Ain spring was cut off, depriving the rest of the city of water. This was a reason for the return of the water carriers.

At the beginning of the 20th century, transport was on donkeys, mules, and horses. As roads were gradually paved, motorcars started to be used. At that time, the main commercial center was still in the Old City. The marketplace was divided into various markets, each specializing in one kind of merchandise. Souq al-Ladadweh was for cereals and sugar; Souq al-Bazar for vegetables; the butchers market for meat; Souq al-'Attarin for herbs; Souq Khan al-Zayt for other various groceries; the rug market, Souq al-Dibagha for leather; Haret al-Nasara (in the Christian Quarter) for wooden and mother-of-pearl works that were sold to tourists, as well as clothes and shoe shops; Souq al-Sagha for gold and jewels; and Bab al-'Amud for dairy products. Traditionally, every market was the specialty of certain families by inheritance.

Women from nearby villages used to sit at the entrance of Bab al-'Amud to sell their produce. Baskets made of bamboo were used for carrying daily provisions from the market. There were small ones that a customer could carry by hand, or large ones that had to be carried by a porter on his back. If a very large amount of provisions was bought, one could hire a porter with a donkey. Most of the porters with donkeys were from nearby villages. As construction outside the wall increased, porters started to have carts or trolleys that they pushed with their hands or pulled with their donkeys.

One of the markets that has lost its prominence these days is that of medical herbs. Before the advent of modern medicine, herbalists used to treat people with their various herbs and herbal extracts. People had great faith in herbalists who were able to treat many minor illnesses. Although herbal shops are now reappearing throughout the world, they have almost disappeared in Jerusalem.

Adjacent to the herbal marketplace was the meat market, where all kinds of meat were sold. Slaying the animals (lambs, goats, cattle, and camels) used to take place at the old slaughterhouse, which was used by Muslims, Christians, and Jews. The Jews in particular had their special rituals for slaying animals, for a Jew is not allowed to eat meat unless it has been slain according to Jewish rituals. With the slightest mistake committed in the process of slaying, the slain animal will be sold to non-Jews at a low price. Before the appearance of motor cars, slain animals were carried by porters on their backs to the meat market. The animal intestines used to be cut off and placed in a tin to be sold separately. In 1936, fighters against the British colonialists used to smuggle small arms in these tins underneath animal intestines. As their smell was repellent, British soldiers would avoid searching them. But eventually this trick was discovered and such tins had to be emptied to show what was beneath the intestines.

As kitchen pots in the past were made of brass, the brass market, located right next to the meat market, thrived. Linked to this was another craft that specialized in polishing the inside of brass pots to get rid of the green patina called verdigris. This latter craft has almost vanished as brass for cooking pots is no longer in vogue, despite the fact that this metal has recently been proven better for the health than aluminum or galvanized metal pots.

The cotton market was another interesting market, as all mattresses and bed covers were made at that market (from cotton or wool), and old mattresses were renewed there. Today, with the availability of readymade furniture, this market has lost its old demand, but it still has a few customers. When fezzes became popular in the cities, shops that specialized in ironing fezzes were established, but they have vanished with the disappearance of this head cover.

The Friday market was a most important one. It was attended by villagers who bought and sold domestic animals. After the 1967 Israeli occupation, this market was closed down.

Another craft that provided only a low income was working as a stone-mason. Stones have been the most popular building blocks used in construction, due to their abundance in Palestine. This craft of working with stones was of two kinds, either cutting stones from the mountains with dynamite, or shaping already cut stones to be suitable for building. The latter was an artistic craft; I often found myself watching the craftsmen work during my youth. As I gazed at these chiselers I would listen to their beautiful rhythms as they engraved their stones under the hot sun. It was also interesting the way they had their meals together. Every one of them would open the food parcel they had brought from home, and all of them would eat together. Their meals were very simple, mostly composed of bread, olives, tomatoes, and onions. If one of them had failed to bring his food, he would be invited to share food with the others. This craft has almost disappeared, as stones nowadays are bought ready cut and given their texture by machines. Large buildings have replaced small houses and, with a neighborhood of various kinds of people living in apartments, residents have been deprived of personal freedom. Modernity has turned lively houses into compact apartments that sometimes lack even balconies. One of the interesting customs in the old days took place when the roof was built. Laborers used to carry building materials up while singing traditional songs that helped keep them active. When the roof was completed, the owner of the house would slay a lamb, stain the front wall with its blood, and distribute its meat among the laborers.

After the Israeli occupation of the Old City and the rest of Palestine in 1967, economic and social conditions changed dramatically. Commerce in the Old City shrank and became limited to small variety shops and selling souvenirs of the Holy Land. It was a pity the Israelis allowed small vehicles and cars into the Old City, as these have become a source of noise and pollution, to say nothing about the many accidents caused.

The traditional mother of pearl and olive wood industry expanded from the influx of pilgrims, mostly Muslims or Christians, into the city, who would buy well crafted souvenirs of their visit. This craft, though internationally well-known, was not the only industry in Jerusalem at the turn of the 20th century. Though it is true that some old industries have disappeared, some are still there. The traditional industries of Jerusalem and elsewhere included: olive and sesame oil pressing, soap, mother-of-pearl and woodworks, flour mills, leather tanning, textiles, shoemaking, tile making, pottery, and embroidery.

In the old days laborers were given low pay and had no social security, which forced them to live in poverty in miserable quarters. However, thanks to traditionally merciful social norms, the poor were never neglected by the rich or by society in general. As traditional industries used low technological standards, the owners, who had inherited their skills from their ancestors, used to supervise the work that was executed by unskilled laborers. With time, modern industries replaced the old and more rights were granted to the working force. Again, the Israeli occupation of the rest of Palestine in 1967 had a generally bad effect on all traditional Palestinian industries for many reasons. For instance, high taxes were imposed, security procedures became tight, and they faced severe and unfair competition from Israeli industries. One of the negative actions taken by the occupation authorities was forcing tourist guides to sit for a test before being allowed to take the job. This deprived many Arab guides of their jobs, because in the test they were required to learn and tell tourists that all historical sites of Palestine were originally Jewish, which they considered a falsification of history and refused to do.

The old communal baths, al-Shifa and al-'Ain, that enjoyed a great popularity in the old days, have closed down.

Manual shoemaking is another craft that has disappeared. In the old days, ready-made shoes were cheap and of low quality and only poor people bought them, whereas wealthier people had their shoes made for them by hand. Alongside shoemaking was the craft of repairing shoes. It was done either by specialized craftsmen or by the shoemakers themselves for their customers. There were shops for repairing shoes, but there were also cobblers who moved through the city with their kits, repairing shoes on the spot.

Naturally, barbershops, where men had their hair cut and faces shaved, have always been there. An important sign of manhood, moustaches were given special care and trimmed into various models. Barbers also used to perform other jobs, the most important of which was circumcision for newborn boys. Hairdressers' shops for women were only in the European Jewish quarters and were not attended by Arab women. Women hairdressers used to visit their customers at home to style their hair, especially for weddings and other occasions. After the 1950s, hairdressers' shops serving women increased in number. Barbers in the old days, and nowadays too, were known for being garrulous, perhaps because they were in a position to know people's news in town through their not less talkative customers.

Tourism has always been the most important source of income for the people of Jerusalem. At the turn of the 20th century, modern hotels were few. But there were a good number of old hotels, called *khans*, which catered to visitors and their riding animals. The 1967 occupation badly affected Arabs working in the tourist industry in the city, where an immediate result of the occupation was a decrease in the number of Arab guides, Arab-owned hotel rooms, souvenir shops, and travel agencies.

CHAPTER ELEVEN: ECONOMIC TRADITIONS

As mentioned before, members of almost all crafts used to elect a leader called sheikh who was officially authenticated at the *Shari'a* court. Nowadays, modern syndicates representing the various professions have superseded the old traditions.

Before the Old City was provided with electricity in the 1930s, streets and houses were lit with gasoline lamps. Cooking was also done on gasoline burners, as butane gas burners were still unknown. Some people also used to cook on charcoal, and a few cooked over firewood. Gasoline burners needed frequent maintenance, which gave rise to the craft of repairing these burners. Some of these technicians had shops, but many used to carry their kits in a wooden box and go around to houses to provide their service on the spot. In fact, those roaming technicians, as well as peddlers, gave a special taste to the city with their beautifully tuned calls in the streets.

Early in the morning, another sort of special tunes were heard: the sounds emitted by the hooves and bells of mules and donkeys, as villagers drove them into the city carrying their loads of vegetables and fruits and unloading them at Bab al-'Amud or Bab al-Khalil. Some of these villagers would sell their load to wholesalers, but others, with the objective of making more money, would sell their produce directly to the customers.

Milk was also sold early in the morning, either from steel containers used to measure out what was wanted by the customer, or milked on the spot from the goat or ewe by a shepherd who chose to drive his herd around the city houses.

Peddlers of boiled eggs and *falafel* sandwiches also had a share in the early morning voices. Their usual customers were school pupils and early laborers, particularly those coming from villages.

Other morning criers were newspaper peddlers. The two major papers in Palestine were *Falastin* and *Al-Difa'* (Defense). Some of those peddlers had the habit of commenting on the news, particularly bad news, with amusing expressions shouted at the top of their voices.

Prior to the 1948 Nakba, at the inside corner of Bab al-'Amud was stationed the famous Hajja Fatima, an African woman who sold delicious roasted nuts, kept fresh and hot in a small tin roaster with fragrant smoke spewing out of a tiny chimney.

Traditionally, the streets of Jerusalem, whether in the old city or the new, were immaculately clean, in spite of the primitive means of collecting garbage in the old days. Garbage collectors used to go from house to house, carrying sacks on their backs, in which they would empty the garbage cans collected from the houses. In addition to whatever food or money homemakers used to give away to garbage collectors, they used to make money selling any saleable material they found in the garbage. Unfortunately, after the 1967 occupation, the municipality imposed high taxes on people for the collection of garbage, and the standard of cleanliness deteriorated.

I cannot complete the character of the city without adding a gypsy color to its morning. Gypsies specializing in selling and sharpening knives and other simple steel utensils roamed through the city. Other peddlers would barter kitchen utensils with used clothes. Bargaining was expected in this exchange of benefits, but a homemaker would be happy at the end if she got rid of unwanted clothes for needed utensils. These bartered old clothes were sold at al-Bashoura Market or, if made of wool, they might be teased and used in making mattresses. In the afternoon the ice-cream vendors had their turn, going through the streets, carrying their sweet refreshments in tight boxes with a belt that they held on their shoulders as they shouted out their merchandise. Some ice-cream vendors used a cart for this purpose. The competitors of the ice-cream vendors sold lupini beans, green chickpeas, fava beans, and corn to those kids who might prefer salty snacks. Lovers of hard sweets would seek out the vendors of *haris*, a sweet made of semolina and saturated with syrup. Another sweet delicacy, cheap enough to suit children, was *baluza* that was made of starch, water, and sugar, with the added taste of vanilla.

Compared to other cities, and due to the spirit of social cooperation among people, beggars in Jerusalem were small in number. In the old days, there was a *takiyya*, which was a place where poor people, as well as strangers to the city, could eat free of charge. Most beggars were strangers who came to the city and, for some reason or another, were unable to go back to where they had come from. They used to be seen mostly at religious places or at cemeteries during public feasts. The strangest justification for begging was when a pilgrim claimed to be well off, but that he had taken a vow to carry no money but beg for what he needed during his pilgrimage to the Holy Land.

In the old days another phenomenon was seen in the city; people with a kind of dementia roamed the streets. Sometimes they were dangerous to children, especially when the latter provoked them. Many vain attempts were made to keep them off the streets. However, some people would take care of them out of religious motives.

Traditional Palestinian costume

12.
The Permanent Jerusalem Carnival

LIKE MANY OTHER ANCIENT CITIES, Jerusalem has inherited many civilizations. Standing at one of its gates in the 1930s or 1940s, one would be amazed by the various fashions worn by passers-by, in spite of the fact that all those people originated from Jerusalem or its environs. These fashions were but the reflections of various historical factors, so it was not difficult for a person from Jerusalem to tell the social status of each person and from where he or she originated.

The first factor that helped shape Palestinian costumes was their use as a social marker. These costumes were a true expression of gender, social status, and class. Many of the costumes go back about 4,500 years to the time of the Canaanites, who were skilled in the paint and textile industries, as well as in embroidery. As the style of Canaanite embroidery was adopted by the Christian monks, these designs reached the far horizons of the world. The embroidered dress, with its various colors and designs, has been the traditional dress of Palestinian women for a long time. Men, on the other hand, traditionally wore Arab dress, with the *kufiyya* as a head cover. In Jerusalem, during the first few decades of the 20th century, no changes had taken place in the traditional costumes, particularly those of men. The men's dress, called *dimayah* or *qunbaz*, is open at the front, with the left side overlapping the right side and both sides are tied to each other on the inside with a thin rope. On the outside, the *qunbaz* was tied with a belt of various designs reflecting the social status of the man. Men of high status had a wide belt of colored silk, inside which a watch was kept, together with the box of snuff. The rich used to bolster their prestigious look by carrying an expensive cane. Below the robe, a pair of baggy white trousers was worn. Instead of the *kufiyya*, old people in particular wore the *'imama*. It was made of various colors and shapes. Turbans are thought to be of ancient Assyrian and Egyptian origin. Under the Ottoman domain, the *tarbush* (fez), which is thought to go back to the Mamlouk era in Egypt (1250-1517), was worn particularly by government officials in Jerusalem and other cities. Common people of the cities wore a *taqiyya*, a small cap that looks like an inverted bowl, made of wool, cotton, or silk. It was worn alone or under the *kufiyya*.

The British occupation of the country after World War One had a tangible effect on dress. Government employees, as well as laborers working at the military camps, started wearing European trousers and jackets like the British. However, during the 1936 revolution, men in Palestinian cities returned to the habit of wearing the *kufiyya*, as a challenge to the British authorities, who were arresting men wearing this headdress. This action perplexed the authorities, but it was simply a gesture of support for the revolution. Children sang amusing songs disparaging those who refused to wear the *kufiyya*. In 1947 and 1948, the *kufiyya* was again used as headwear for the fighters; and again after 1967, when it became a token of resistance to occupation.

The pious Ashkenazis (immigrant European Jews) had a special black costume, with a black European hat and long braids and beard, which stood out against the indigenous environment of the city and the whole region. After the 1967 occupation, Orthodox Jews, often aggressively nationalist, might also be seen toting machine guns.

Naturally, as menswear was subject to change, so was women's wear. The traditional country dress of women slightly differed from one region to another in Palestine and the design and colors of the embroidery on her dress also differed from one village to another. When countrywomen came to Jerusalem to sell their produce or to buy their needs, one could tell which village they had come from by listening to their accent or looking at their dress. With the development of society, especially as young countrywomen went to school and wore school uniforms, the new generation gradually abandoned traditional dress, except on special occasions like weddings.

For quite a long time, the Ottoman effect on city women was apparent, not only in Palestine, but in all cities of the region, particularly Greater Syria. Until the first half of the 20th century, with the exception of most Christian women, city women in Palestine, when they went out of the house, had to wear a black robe that covered their whole body from head to foot. This kind of dress for women became popular during the Ottoman era on the false grounds of conforming to Islamic traditions. As a result of schooling and the increase in educational standards, women gradually freed themselves from this ultra-conservative dress, but not after natural resistance from conservative society. This kind of robe was also worn by a few Christian women. In 1936, as the British soldiers dared not search women, this ultra-conservative dress served a good purpose in the revolt, namely to smuggle ammunition to the revolutionaries or to give the men the opportunity to hide dressed in a woman's robe. When this was discovered, the British used women to do the searching. One amusing anecdote from this time told of a man dressed as a woman with the end of his trousers appearing from below the robe. A passer-by who noticed him said, "Take care of your clothes, woman!" The man, of course, understood the hint and hitched up his trousers better. The women of al-Khalil (Hebron) who used to live in Jerusalem or came as visitors had their own dress. They used to wear a blue skirt that covered their lower body, together with a white dress that covered from her head to the middle part of her body.

The Jewish families who lived in the Old City used to wear European dress. Religious Ashkenazi women used to wear dresses that covered the whole body. Sometimes we used to notice that their hair below the head covering was shaved, apparently for religious reasons. Outside the Old City, Jewish women used to wear ordinary European dress, in fact, some of them wore short trousers.

Some songs appeared describing the exciting dress of Jewish women, suggesting that they were used by Zionists to seduce Arab men.

In their dress, Christian women were not much different from Muslim women, but, with them, change was faster from traditional to contemporary dress. In this context the robes worn by nuns when they moved from one church to another should also be mentioned. During religious occasions, their number increased as well as the number of pilgrims coming from various countries. Pilgrims, both Muslim and Christian, had always given Jerusalem a cosmopolitan look that might not be seen anywhere else. Unfortunately, the spirit of Jerusalem nowadays, due to the Israeli occupation, is almost gone. One can easily discern the sorrow in the eyes of Palestinians everywhere in the city. In fact, the Israelis who occupied Palestine have frequently taken over Palestinian traditions of food and dress, claiming them as their own.

13.
The Tower of Babylon

JERUSALEM HAS A UNIQUE CHARACTER, inherited from its ancient Arab-Canaanite history. This has given it a strong immunity against any change that might contradict its historical identity. The most recent test has been the Israeli occupation of the city in 1967. Great efforts have been exerted by the Israelis to change the Arab identity of the city. The best that has been achieved so far was an increase in the number of settlements around the city on confiscated land, where typically only Jews are allowed to live. The Arab-Islamic tradition that gave Jerusalem its character has been a civilization of tolerance which accepts all religions and races, with all their different habits. Jerusalem is like the Tower of Babel, which is said to have gathered together many different people speaking different languages and having different habits. The people of Jerusalem have had to be tolerant for throughout history they have welcomed to their city all kinds of pilgrims and visitors from every corner of the world.

Shopkeepers had to speak many languages to be able to communicate with their foreign customers and make them feel at home. After Saladin liberated Jerusalem from the Crusaders, many different people came to live in the city, forming different communities, with separate habits and languages. Eventually, these communities adopted the Arab-Islamic character of the city and spoke Arabic. The places where some of these foreign communities lived still keep their names, like the Italian Hospital Area Quarter (al-Tilyaniyya), the German Colony (Koloniyyat al-Alman), the American Colony (al-koloniyya al-Amrikiyyah), and al-Maskobiyya (the Russian Quarter).

Many of the areas were from Islamic nations: al-Bukharia (Afghan's Corner) and Naqshabandiyya (Indian Corner), to name two.

There were also foreign schools and foreign religious institutions, both Muslim and Christian, like Terra Sancta College, College de la Salle, Saint George School, Schneller School, and Schmidt School. In addition, one can notice from the names of some Jerusalem families that they refer to almost all Arab countries or cities, like Masri (Egyptian), Maghribi (Northwest African countries, as well as Andalusia), Shami (Damascene), Dimyati (of Dimyat, an Egyptian city), Sudani, Iraqi, Yamani, and Kurdi.

As a result of Ottoman rule, some people had Turkish titles, like *afandi* and *baik*. Such titles were usually granted to officials of high rank. The villagers used to attach the title *afandi* to all city dwellers, especially if they wore European dress. Nowadays, some of these Ottoman titles are unofficially attached to names of people as a way of showing respect, but sometimes in a joking way. There was another Ottoman title, *pasha*, given by a royal decree only to high-ranking officials and military officers. Women in high society had the unofficial title of *khanum* or *hanum*. After Ottoman rule, these titles were officially stopped, but continued to be used unofficially. Eventually, people came to prefer using the Arab titles of *Sayyed* or *Ustadh* for Sir. *Khawaja* was the generic name for any foreigner (usually European), but it was also used for mocking an Arab imitating foreigners. Some Arab families have inherited Turkish titles, like *Agha* or *Khazendar*. Given names in different periods may reflect the names of famous leaders or politicians of the time. During Ottoman rule, names like Tharwat and Jawdat were in vogue; those names, though of Arabic origin, were names of prominent Ottoman officials.

During World War II, some people gave their children German names, like Hitler and Rommel, on the grounds that the Germans were fighting the British who were encouraging Jewish immigration to Palestine. More recently, names like Jihad (struggle), Thawra (revolution), Hurriyya (freedom), and 'Awdah have been given to babies born after the 1948 Nakba. Names of some Palestinian towns and villages have also been given to babies, like Bisan, Safad, Yafa, and Haifa. Such use of political or lost place names shows the general state of mind of the people. Apart from these kinds of names, short names, like Rana, Suha, Lama, and Fadi have become in vogue these days.

CHAPTER THIRTEEN; THE TOWER OF BABYLON

Jerusalem c. 1940s

14.
Folk Medicine

MODERN MEDICINE HAS MADE EXTRAORDINARY developments in the recent decades and cannot be compared to medical knowledge at the beginning of the 20th century. From my practice of medicine in Jerusalem, Kuwait, and Jordan, I have noticed that a good number of people still believe in the old folk medicine, or what we call Arab medicine. This folk medicine depends on concoctions and herbal extracts, which are given to patients on the basis of knowledge acquired by personal or inherited experience. Some believers in folk medicine are convinced that it gives better results than modern medicine. Naturally, one can not ask people to follow scientific methods in order to prove the truth of their belief. However, we must admit the power of belief in curing illnesses. This is perhaps what happens with many people treated by herbalists.

In the past, people, both Muslim and Christian, believed that demons were the direct cause of illness and treatment was based on scaring away the demons from a sick human body. Simple as they were, people in the past refrained from visiting a house with a sick child, fearing that the demon causing the illness was likely to attack them. One of their beliefs was that a woman should not be admitted into a house with children during her period, as she might transmit a disease to them. Bad *jinnis*, female demons (*qarinas*), and the evil eye were believed to be the cause of illness, too. That is why magic and certain religious rituals were believed to be good remedies for the sick. The *qarina* was believed to keep looking for children to hurt them. That included those still inside their mother's womb. People also believed that demons might go around camouflaged in the form of humans, especially during festivals. The means to be protected against demons was by asking a "server of God" to make an amulet, either for treatment or prevention (prophylaxis, in modern medical jargon!). In the case of children, changing of the name of the child was a means to confuse the *qarina* and make her lose her way to the victim.

In this context we notice that people also had sayings that showed good insight in avoiding diseases, like the following:

> A gram of prevention is better than a ton of treatment!
> When your head aches, feed it, when your stomach aches, deprive it!
> Eat with an infidel, but not with a person with long nails!
> A house that the sun enters does not need a doctor!
> Change of air is better than medicine!
> Staying up late at night is like gangrene for the bones!
> Cold is the cause of all illness!
> Cold in summer is sharper than a sword!

People also resorted to amulets to keep away demons that specialized in love and hatred. A woman whose husband did not show her love, for example, or who thinks of divorcing her, will ask a "server of God" to make an amulet for her. The amulet maker may ask the women to put the amulet in the husband's clothes without him noticing. The logic behind this was that someone has concocted a kind of magic either against the wife, with the purpose of hurting her, or toward the husband, with the purpose of winning his heart.

In my childhood, my grandmother used to treat a child suffering from vomiting and diarrhea by massaging its belly with hot olive oil. Then she would make a piece of dough, mix it with olive oil, apply it to the child's belly, and ask the mother to give him/her a warm infusion of sage or chamomile. For cuts, coffee powder or ash was applied to the wound to stop the bleeding. Burns were treated by applying egg whites and a bee sting was treated with garlic.

When a child was scared of something, he or she is given water in what was called the "scare bowl," which was believed to have the power of dissipating one's fears. This brass bowl, which pilgrims bring from Mecca, has Qur'anic verses and Arabesque ornaments engraved on the inside as well as the outside. In his work on folk customs, Dr. Tawfiq Kanaan was able to trace many of these habits back to ancient times in the region. Before Islam, these bowls had horoscopes engraved on them instead of Qur'anic verses. The origin of these magical bowls, according to Dr. Kanaan, is that *jinnis* used them for their baths. One day, a *jinni* had his bath at a spring, and when he left the place, he forgot to take his bowl with him. A lucky passerby found the bowl and in a few days he discovered its merits. The bowls that people have now are merely copies of the original.

For treating sprained arms or legs, certain men and women were known for their massaging skills. When I was a teenager I sprained my wrist while playing volleyball, and my mother took me to Hajja Umm Jalal, a well-known masseuse at the time. She massaged my wrist, then applied a piece of dough mixed with olive oil and an egg, and instructed me not to take it off for two weeks. A few hours later, I felt pain, but my parents thought I must bear it. A few days later, a bad smell came from my wrist, but my parents thought it was from the egg in the dough. A couple of days after that, pus oozed out of my wrist. When I took off the dough I found a lot of pus covering a large area. This prompted my parents to take me to a doctor, who reprimanded me, and blamed my parents for taking me to a masseuse instead of a doctor. Later, when I practiced medicine, I made use of this scar to convince my patients of the importance of going to a specialist. In Arabic we say, "Asking someone with experience is better than asking a doctor." So I would say to my patients, "I'm both, someone with experience as well as a doctor!"

People in the past considered envy to be a great devil that could cause most diseases. During my childhood, when a child had a fever or caught a cold, the first thing his or her mother would do was to remember who among the women who had recently seen the child looked with an envious eye and caused the illness. The next step, after that superstitious diagnosis, was to start reading some verses from the holy book. How strange it was that other people might envy us when we were as good and as bad as all other children. If the situation was grave, burning incense, coupled with readings from the holy book, would be a must. If these homemade rituals were not enough, then Sheikh 'Atef al-Dissi, a well-known *darwish* in the city, would be called to perform his more effective rituals. After performing the rituals, Sheikh 'Atef would give the patient an amulet made of a triangular piece of cloth, with hidden script written by him inside. We never had the courage to open the amulet and see its contents. In my childhood, I had an amulet that was always attached with a pin to the inside of my shirt. A blue bead with a lump of alum was also popular for preventing envy. Beads are usually pinned to exposed places and to clothing, either alone or with an amulet.

Beads, in the old days, had many popular purposes. The bead of love and luck was a precious thing that a woman would keep and only give to her daughter or granddaughter. Apparently ancient people believed blue beads had the power of goodness, for it was thought to distract envious eyes and disable their power of envy. Arabs in general have black or brown eyes, so blue eyes were a symbol of strangers. There is a saying that common people recall when describing an envious person, "His eyes are blue and his teeth are set apart!"

Part of the reason why people used to go to herbalists and Sufis to treat their ailments was the prevalence of poverty. With the great number of political prisoners from all walks of life in the 1930s, many families lost their breadwinner. This made it difficult for people to find the means to cover the expenses of medical treatment. Besides, doctors in the early 1930s were few. One of the doctors in Jerusalem was Dr. Tawfiq Kanaan, who became well known for his free treatment of the poor. We were told that he used to go on his mule to the villages around Jerusalem to treat poor villagers. Well-to-do villagers paid him in eggs, chickens, and sometimes lambs. Another benefactor was Dr. Husam Abu'l-Sa'ud, whose good reputation for taking care of the poor was an example for me in my career. Apart from foreign missionary clinics, the Islamic Infirmary was the only national medical institution in Jerusalem that offered free services to the public.

Many herbs, whether local or imported, were used for various kinds of ailments. Herbalists in Jerusalem had their marketplace in the Old City where they practiced their craft in small shops filled with all kinds of herbs they prescribed and sold to their patients. Although treatment with herbs is now an important subject of research at modern universities with new, beneficial discoveries, this kind of treatment in the old days was not always successful. A curious remedy for pneumonia, in addition to taking honey with lemon and ginger, was applying hot olive oil to the chest, over which a perforated newspaper was placed, and the patient was kept warm in bed. Medically, of course, that was not enough. When patients came to me astonished that the treatment did not work, I would jokingly tell them that either they had chosen the wrong newspaper, or that the news in that paper was bad. In general, apart from the fact that some old practices of medicine were strange, and in some cases dangerous, many herbal remedies were good, especially in mild cases. An example of home treatment that is still used these days is taking minced garlic in yogurt for diarrhea, or drinking water boiled with the peel of a pomegranate. Sage for mild stomach pains also gives good results. Thyme is a popular herb in Palestine that is used in various recipes as food or as a remedy. Modern research has found that thyme has many good benefits.

Barbers also played a part in medical treatment. Circumcision and extraction of painful teeth were their specialties, together with using leeches. In this regard, there have been new medical reports that claim good results using leeches in the reduction of pain due to rheumatoid arthritis. Leeches were used for sucking blood, but modern research has found a benefit in the secretions of the leech when placed on the skin.

What is called *hijama* (cupping) in Arabic was also popular. This old treatment is performed with special cups of glass that had a conical shape. The cups are placed on the back or the chest of the patient and a piece of paper is burned inside the glass so that the oxygen inside is consumed, rendering the pressure outside higher than the one inside, which makes the glass stick to the patient. Usually the skin where the cup is placed is slightly, but carefully, cut so that blood may ooze out by difference in pressure. This was the treatment of choice for colds suffered in the cold winters of Jerusalem. *Hijama* is an ancient Arab treatment mentioned in traditional books of medicine as a good treatment for rheumatism, backache, inflamed joints, headache, insomnia, irritated colon, sciatica, chronic cough, lung diseases and constipation.

In the 1930s and 1940s, pharmacists were a trusted source for remedies and had numerous patients seeking advice. This is still the case today. Pharmacists in the past, in addition to their knowledge as college graduates, were also well known for their good manners. Very few medicines were ready-made, and almost all medicines were prepared at the pharmacy. Due to this fact, a patient had to wait for some time while the pharmacist prepared his medicine on the spot. Locally prepared medicines were much cheaper than imported ready-made ones. Still, patients at that time often complained of the high price the pharmacist charged. Certain popular medicines, like gripe water, iodine tincture, and some cough syrups, were prepared and stocked, to be sold over the counter. Giving injections was another service pharmacies offered.

Midwives, as mentioned earlier, enjoyed great respect, especially in the villages. In addition to helping mothers give birth, they treated certain feminine ailments, successfully or otherwise. There were two kinds of midwives: the legally licensed ones, who had official training in midwifery and were officially recognized by the health authorities, and local ones who had gained experience by practice, perhaps as an apprentice with an older midwife. Some of the local midwives were later tested and licensed by the health authorities, but were considered practical midwives and given a lower status than the former. Eventually, mothers preferred going to hospitals and avoiding the hassle of finding a midwife and bringing her home.

Patients with diseases that had not been discovered and could not be cured by simple domestic remedies, like cancer and psychiatric illnesses, used to try all kinds of available treatment with no results. Following the old Arab saying, "Cauterizing is the last remedy," desperate patients would try this remedy, harsh as it was. Cauterizing, it must be mentioned, was not practiced by the people of Jerusalem. One had to go to the villages or to the Bedouin community where it was practiced. Sometimes, unscientific as such a practice might be, it had positive results, either psychological or because the patient was recovering anyway. When cauterizing failed, as it did most of the time, then sorcerers and fortune-tellers were the only stars in a black night. A few sorcerers and fortune-tellers were known in Jerusalem before 1948; later the number decreased. The most famous went by the name of Abul-Fijl, who had a kind of "clinic" in the Old City, with a large sign giving his titles, experience, and qualifications, describing him as a specialist in astrology, asterism, deactivation of magic, and making amulets. The list was long, indeed, and the sorcerer would usually demand something that belonged to the person for whom the magic was being concocted, even something as small as a few hairs, nail cuttings, or a piece of his clothes. In the case of hair, if the person was a man, his barber might be asked to help. Then the magic was activated, either in the form of an amulet or as a preparation that had to be added to the person's food or drink.

Fortune-telling was much in vogue at the beginning of the 20th century. The purpose was to get knowledge of something unknown, like the news of a loved one who had gone away and not returned, or to find out who had committed a theft. One of the popular ways of telling a fortune was called *mandal*. It does not seem to be practiced any more, unless on a limited scale. An amount of olive oil, sometimes simply water, was put on a plate that was placed in front of the practitioner and the customer, who would have done his ablution and promised to tell the truth. Both the fortune-teller and the customer held the plate, or the customer placed his hand in the liquid. The fortune-teller would fall into a trance and utter some words, after which he started slowly whispering, as if to someone inside the plate, explaining the problem and requesting information about it. He looked as if he could see images inside the oil. He would tell whatever information he received: if the person had asked about a theft, then he might give a description of the thief or the court proceedings. The customer would be pleased with the information he received and happily pay the fee. Fortune-telling was also done by reading a cup of Arab coffee after it is drunk by the person whose fortune is to be told. The cup is placed upside down on its saucer to have whatever remaining liquid dry out, leaving the coffee residue that makes shapes on the inside wall of the cup. The fortune-teller interpreted these shapes to bear information on the person's fortune. Fortune-telling by a cup of coffee is still practiced by many people, particularly women, albeit privately and most of the time for fun.

Making Kataayef during Ramadan

15.
Food and Cuisine

PEOPLE OF JERUSALEM, AS WELL AS ALL PEOPLE of Greater Syria, have inherited their cuisine from their Canaanite forefathers, and have developed it through time, being influenced by the various civilizations that passed through the region throughout history. Turkish cuisine perhaps had the biggest effect, for the Sultan's palace, not so far from the Syrian territories, was a central melting pot of the various cuisines practiced in the countries under the Ottoman Empire.

At the beginning, Arab food in the desert depended mainly on dates and milk, together with mutton and lamb. In agricultural areas, people planted wheat and other cereal grains, together with vegetables and fruits. Over time, with increasing populations, large villages developed into towns. These developments were naturally accompanied by continuous changes in food, clothes, and habits.

In any traditional house in old Jerusalem, one could see a great resemblance to Canaanite houses: a large ceramic/earthenware jar filled with drinking water with a cup over it for drinking, a hand mill for grinding grain, a fine and a coarse sieve, a mortar made of iron or brass, a baking pan (*saj*), dried produce like garlic and okra, hung up in a corner in the house, a low table (*tabliyya*) for taking meals, and various cooking pots, the bottoms of which would be blackened with soot from firewood.

All these utensils were inherited from one generation to another and gradually developed to suit changing living conditions. These days most households have modern equipment.

At meals, all members of the family would gather together. According to the family size, food was served on trays or large plates and people ate either with their hands or with spoons directly from the tray; the habit of each person having their own plate was still unknown.

With the increase in the number of families, followed by an increase in the city size, and young married couples preferring to live independently, rather than in a room at the family house, families lost an important social cohesion. With the higher standard of education and women leaving the house for work, fast food has replaced family meals and helped weaken family ties.

Bread has always been the major constituent of the Palestinian meal. The ancient Canaanites considered wheat a sacred substance. The fact that bread, as food and nutrition, was of great importance in early history, can be seen from the Christian "Lord's prayer" beseeching God to "give us our daily bread."

Fresh legumes such as lentils, peas, and chickpeas used to be dried and stored in special pots in the storage rooms of old houses. The storage room, which maintained a cool temperature during the summer heat, had large alcoves in the wall for storing legumes, ghee, oil, and other food items.

Jerusalem cuisine benefited from rich and varied domestic produce, as well as from native plants like mallow, and wild herbs of the mountains and valleys like sage, thyme, and chamomile. This gave rise to aphorisms that expressed the benefits of such produce, like "With figs no bread" and "With watermelon no cooking."

The Old City lacked the green areas necessary for even small-scale agriculture, but most households planted mint and thyme in pots and raised some chickens for laying eggs. Outside the city wall, there was abundant opportunity to plant vegetables, fruit, olives, and lemons. Some people raised sheep and chickens.

Winter in Jerusalem is very cold and snow sometimes falls. Before refrigerators were available, people used to preserve food and store it at home to be used in severe weather. The following are foods that were often preserved:

Okra (bamia): Okra was tied together with thread in the shape of a necklace and dried in the sun, then hung in the storeroom or kitchen.
Jew's Mallow: (Mulukhiyya): The leaves were dried in the sun and kept in sacks to be used when needed.
Tomatoes: The tomato was cut into two pieces, salted, and dried in the sun. When immersed in hot water, it became fresh again and could be used for salad. Another way of preserving tomatoes was to make tomato paste. It was partially dried in the sun, stored in glass pots, and used for cooking.
Green beans, fava beans, and sweet peas: The ripe seeds (beans) were dried and stored.
Garlic: The whole plant was hung to dry in the kitchen or in the house yard and used gradually.
Yogurt: Yogurt was placed in a sack of linen and hung to allow its water to drain out. When it was half-dry, it was made into small balls, sometimes after the addition of table salt, and kept immersed in olive oil in a glass pot. In this shape it is called *labaneh*. Another dried yogurt, called *kishk* or *jamid*, was made by taking the half-dried yogurt, shaping it into larger balls, and fully drying it in the sun on some straw. At the time of cooking, it was soaked in water.
Fruit: Various fruits were preserved by drying. Grapes and figs were simply dried as is, while apples and apricots were dried with sugar. Some fruits were boiled with sugar to make jam.
Meat: Meat was also dried, but it required experience. Fish was salted in a special way that also needed expertise.

Other products were also made at home, like vinegar and pickles. A good homemaker, no matter how poor her family was, could always find cheap, but nourishing food for her family like lentil soup and *mujaddara* (made of lentils and rice or lentils and cracked wheat).

Furniture was simple. In the kitchen, there was a cupboard called *namliyya* that had two compartments; the upper one had a door covered with a metallic mesh to allow ventilation and prevent flies and other insects from getting in. The lower compartment was for storing food, like oil, ghee, and legumes. An insulated icebox was later added to kitchens for keeping meat and vegetables for a short time, using a block of ice to keep the temperature down. Some of these iceboxes had a water pipe that was connected by one end to the main water pipe, then coiled under the ice, while the other end was connected to a tap that poured cold water for drinking in summer. Ice had to be brought daily from the ice factory.

Before the introduction of kerosene burners, cooking was done with firewood. Later, the kerosene burner became a convenient and relatively clean tool for cooking, heating water for the bath, and baking bread.

In comparison with women today, who have all kinds of modern technology to help them prepare even the most difficult Arab food, women in the past used to sit on the floor at a low wooden table to prepare the family food, much of which demanded time and effort. Today most modern women work outside their houses to earn an additional income for the family. Many Arab dishes, like stuffed vine leaves are difficult to prepare and time-consuming. These dishes are still very much in demand today. Others, which require even more effort such as stuffed sheep entrails, may still be appreciated by many people but very few people know how to prepare them or are willing to exert the effort.

One of the famous dishes in Palestine was *musakhkhan*. As it was usually prepared with olive oil, it was more popular in those regions of Palestine where the olive tree was widely grown and it was especially prepared in autumn, which was the season of olive oil. It was prepared with roasted chicken, together with onion cut into small slices and boiled in olive oil. Traditional bread, which was baked in the special village oven called *tabun*, was used for this dish. The general availability of its ingredients, olive oil, onions, and *tabun* bread, made it a specialty of the villages, where it was presented to important guests. This popular dish is in great demand nowadays and there are restaurants in major cities all over the Arab world that specialize in preparing it.

The towns of al-Khalil (Hebron) and Gaza were famous for *kidra*. This was made of rice, mutton, garlic, chickpeas, and a lot of special spices, cooked in a special pot made of thick brass, or sometimes of strong pottery. The Bedouin have an equally famous dish, called *mansaf*. This was prepared from rice and mutton, and cooked in dried yogurt (*jamid*) that has been soaked in water. *Mansaf* was the food of choice for special occasions, like weddings and funerals. It was presented on trays covered first with a sheet of thin bread, called *shrak*, which was covered with boiled rice and chunks of mutton, then hot *jamid* was poured over the whole dish. Eating *mansaf*, particularly in the old days, had a special protocol. It was eaten directly from the large tray, with the right hand, in such a way as to collect rice with meat and make a small ball of the mixture; the ball is then popped into the mouth without leaving a trace of food on the lips. Obviously, this required good training! Some people in certain villages refrained from eating with their guests, as they took the duty of busying themselves by shredding meat and pouring hot *jamid* if needed. In the old days, the custom was that people would start eating after their elder (sheikh) had started and would stop when he stopped. Like *musakhkhan*, *mansaf* is now prepared in many places outside of Palestine and a few restaurants in major cities have it on their menu as a specialty. More and more people break the protocol of eating *mansaf* with their hand, preferring to eat it in small dishes with a spoon or even with a knife and fork.

Maqluba (literally meaning "upside-down"), a popular and exclusively Palestinian dish, was and is still famous. It is made of rice cooked over mutton and fried eggplants. When it is ready to be served, the cooking pot is turned upside down so that its contents pour onto a tray holding the shape of the pot, with the mutton and eggplant on top of the rice. It is usually served with fried pine nuts and almonds, and with yogurt or salad on the side. Cauliflower or carrots may also be used instead of eggplant. Jerusalemites who served *Maqluba*, instead of the more expensive meat dishes villagers and Bedouins present to their guests, were often mocked. The people of Jerusalem were sometimes mocked for other "stingy" habits as well, and it has been said that they would receive their guests in such a phlegmatic manner that they felt unwelcome. A guest, as the joke goes, would be asked when they would be leaving. According to Arab custom, asking a guest such a question is taboo. It was also said that Jerusalemites would ask their guest, "Will you spend your night with us, or prefer to go to a hotel? Will you have supper with us, or it is healthier to sleep with a light stomach?" It goes without saying that the people of Jerusalem denied these accusations, which were only exaggerations for the sake of poking fun at them. Since Jerusalem was a relatively large metropolitan city, one can not expect its people to have identical habits as those of the villagers or the Bedouin who lead a simple life and can cater more freely to guests. Still, basic habits of hospitality are common among all Arabs, whether city dwellers, villagers, or Bedouins. There is an old Arab saying that goes, "Receive me well and don't give me dinner!" In a most concise way, this saying describes the proper way of receiving guests, with a big smile that shows affection and pleasure. Another saying that expresses people's willingness to receive guests goes like this: "A small house is large enough for a hundred friends." As a guest may be too shy to eat well, old customs stipulated that a guest must be urged to eat more. An amusing expression when the guest affirms his fullness goes like this, "A full person can still have 40 mouthfuls!" This saying may have originated from the fact that some guests left some room for more food intake on the grounds that the host will pressure him or her to eat more. The whole argument between a guest with an overly full stomach and his host is quite funny. In fact, there is a famous wise Arab aphorism that goes, "Stop eating before your stomach is full, for bad consequences come with overfilled stomachs." When a guest finished their meal, there were many traditional expressions with which they thanked their host. Most of these expressions are still used today. Alcoholic drinks were served by Christians only. Muslims would serve fresh juices and lemonades with the meal, as well as water.

At the end of a meal, coffee was a must. Arabic coffee was served without sugar. Turks added sugar to Arabic coffee, hence the name Turkish coffee, which became more popular in the cities, but never superseded Arabic coffee, particularly on serious occasions. In the old days, coffee beans were roasted and ground at home. Nowadays, there are coffee shops where many types of coffee may be found. Such specialized shops have relieved people of the burden of roasting and grinding coffee at home. In the past, serving coffee to the guests had a special protocol. Except in certain cases, Arabic coffee would be served beginning with the person sitting on the right-hand side of the head of the table. When sweetened coffee was introduced, people adopted the habit of giving priority to either the oldest person, or to the most important person. Sweetened coffee was distributed in cups placed on a tray, while Arabic coffee was poured into the cup from the coffee pot that was carried in the server's left hand so that the cup was held and given by the right hand. The guest, or whoever received the cup of coffee, would take it with his right hand. In certain Bedouin societies, the server refused to give the cup of coffee to a person who tried to take it with his left hand. That habit seems to originate from old beliefs that the left hand or side is devilish. When the guest finished his cup and wished to have more, he extended his to the server who refilled it. Otherwise, the guest shook the cup, indicating that he did not want more. Unlike with food, the coffee server did not insist on the guest taking more coffee if the cup was shaken. Generally, however, it was considered unbecoming for a guest to refuse taking at least one sip of coffee. If a guest did not take any coffee, the host would urge him to take it. This was because refusing to take coffee might be a sign from the guest that there was a request to the host. In this case, if the host does not give the guest a positive gesture, the latter will leave without taking his coffee, in which case the problem must be solved according to tradition. Tea, on the other hand, was not commonly served in celebrations and had no special protocol.

In relation to food, there are innumerable sayings in Arabic that express the traditions to be followed and what are acceptable manners. The following are a few of these sayings:

> Feed the mouth and the eye will be shy (indicating that hospitality is a way to bring hearts together, or that the person who eats your food will likely comply with your request);
> Encounter your enemy hungry but not naked (advice on showing power);

Eat the way you like, but dress the way people like;
He who eats a large chunk will choke (advising against greed);
Instead of eating eggplants, cover your naked buttock (because eggplants were a luxury food, this was advice for a person who preferred to eat eggplant rather than buy clothes to cover himself);
Take olive oil and butt the wall (promoting the goodness of olive oil).

There were many inexpensive, popular types of food available in Jerusalem. Bread has always been the most important component of a Palestinian meal. As mentioned above, Canaanites regarded wheat, and therefore bread, as sacred and Arabs had the same respect for bread. People used to be very sensitive about throwing even a small piece of bread into the garbage. Instead, unwanted pieces of bread were dried and stored to be used in certain kinds of food, like soup, or were left on the house roof for the birds to eat. Children were urged, when they saw a piece of bread in the street, to pick it up, kiss it, and put it on a high place for birds to eat.

From ancient times until today, the methods for making bread have passed through numerous stages. Perhaps the oldest traditional bread was called *saj* bread, or *shrak*. The dough was made out of whole-wheat flour, without adding yeast. Then the dough was divided into small balls, each of which was manipulated by the baker's hands into a thin, large, circular loaf, put on a thin convex metal tray, and heated from below by firewood. (Nowadays butane gas is used.) Before using the metal tray, this kind of bread was baked on hot stone. Nowadays, this kind of bread is eaten more by villagers and Bedouins than by city dwellers. However, with the aim of providing a novelty, some fast food restaurants use *saj* bread for sandwiches.

After *saj* (*shrak*) bread, *Tabun* bread became popular. It was also made of whole-wheat flour, but with yeast. The dough in this kind of bread has more water content and the round large loaf was baked in an oven called the *tabun*. The *tabun* was a primitive rural oven that was heated with animal dung, particularly cattle dung that was mixed with straw and dried in the sun. The dung is gathered around the baking compartment of the oven, which was made with special hardened soil, the lower part of which is lined with a loose layer of small *wadi* stones that retain heat. The loaf was put over these heated stones that left small dents in it, giving it a peculiar shape. The baking compartment was covered with a metal lid for a short while until the loaf was baked. Eaten with olive oil, olives, onion, and cheese, this loaf constituted a simple but nourishing meal for the villagers in the field. *Tabun* bread is the major constituent of *musakhan*, a dish mentioned earlier.

In the cities, a new kind of bread, called *kmaj*, became popular. It was much smaller than *saj* and *tabun* and baked in stone bakeries. European bread was also introduced and became popular in certain societies. However, irrespective of its kind, bread remains a major part of every meal.

Perhaps the most popular simple and cheap food, especially in Greater Syria and Egypt, is *falafel*—called *tu'miyya* in Egypt. In Palestine and the whole of Greater Syria it is made of cracked chickpeas, while in Egypt it is made of cracked, dry fava beans. Both are soaked in water with other ingredients that give it a special flavor. When it is ripe and ready, small, round balls are formed from the dough either with the hand or with a special metal tool. Then the balls are deep-fried in olive oil or other plant oils, such as sesame oil. Some people stuff *falafel* with onion and sumac, others dip the ball in sesame seeds before it is fried. The mixture of spices added is considered the specialty of each restaurant, and as usual, restaurant owners keep it a secret. As the cost for starting a *falafel* shop is very small, and the ingredients of *falafel* are also cheap, the cost of a *falafel* meal is affordable to all people. That is why laborers, students, and poor families have depended on *falafel*, taken with tomatoes or onion, as their major, perhaps only, meal. In every quarter there was a *falafel* vendor serving customers from a tiny shop or mobile cart. Many *falafel* vendors who started modestly have grown very rich after a few years of toil. Palestinians took this industry with them to the countries of their Diaspora. What is funny, perhaps sad, is that the Israelis, after the establishment of their state in Palestine, claimed *falafel*, together with other Palestinian folk customs, as an Israeli tradition.

The other popular dish, dubbed "the dinner of the poor," is

hummus. This is a cheap and easy-to-prepare food, composed of well boiled chickpeas, made into a fine paste mixed with water, *tahini* (thick sesame paste), lemon, and garlic. When the *hummus* is done, it is poured into a plate, shaped and artistically ornamented with spices and a few pieces of pickles or cut tomatoes and whole chickpeas. It is then eaten topped with olive oil or, more expensively, with pine nuts fried in butter. To make it even richer, ground meat with fried pine nuts is added. A derivative of *hummus* is called *fattah*. This is made of bread that is well soaked in the boiling water of the chickpeas, mixed with the boiled chickpeas and some yogurt. It is served in small bowls. To enrich it, it is topped with pine nuts fried with butter, alone or with ground meat. *Hummus* vendors have recently had to face competition from canned, ready-to-eat *hummus*, but the quality of canned *hummus* makes one appreciate the real thing even more. Even *falafel* is now available either as canned, ready-made dough that needs to be cut and fried, or as frozen dough already cut into pieces for frying.

The third popular and cheap food is *foul mudammas*, which is composed of well-boiled dried beans made into a thick paste and flavored with garlic, lemon, olive oil, and spices. This dish is more popular in Egypt, but the beans there, unlike the custom in Greater Syria, are not crushed into a paste.

Cheap and popular, *ka'k al-Quds*, as it is called in other Palestinian towns, is a French kind of bread sold in the morning and at noon from mobile carts that are stationed at every busy corner, served with thyme, falafel, or baked eggs. It is a fast, convenient, and cheap meal. As modern "fast food" has only recently come to Jerusalem, this *ka'k* was our fast food, as well as other sandwiches containing *falafel* or other ingredients like roasted spleen and sausage. Kebab was sold at small stands that roasted the meat at the entrance of a shop that usually had no facilities for serving seated customers. Villagers and other visitors of the city used to take their order of kebab in a loaf and eat it outside. People of Jerusalem often took their orders to eat at home, but most people preferred to make their own *kebab* at home on the grounds that the quality of meat at the *souq* might be questionable.

Unfortunately, American fast food restaurants were introduced into the city at the end of the 20th century. It is a trend that seems to be irresistible, despite its social and health-related drawbacks.

Due to difficult economic conditions, people could not afford to eat meat dishes on a daily basis. Daily food in ordinary households in Jerusalem (as well as in other Palestinian towns) came from seasonal vegetables and whatever was stored at home in the way of lentils, beans, cracked wheat, peas, chickpeas, fava beans, dried okra, and *mulukhiyya*, in addition to olive oil, cooking fat, olives, *labaneh*, and thyme. In the city, rice was a major component of most meals. In villages, whole wheat and cracked wheat, the product of Palestinian land, were also eaten often. Lentils were called the meat of the poor, as they are rich in protein and iron. I used to know of certain poor families whose daily food was nothing but lentil soup. They rarely had the chance to eat meat. There were a variety of cheap dishes made of lentils, the most popular of which was *mujaddara*, a dish of lentils and rice or cracked wheat. Rice was also used in other inexpensive dishes containing no meat. One of the cheapest dishes was *qallayet bandoura*, which was prepared mainly from tomatoes with onion and garlic, fried in olive oil, and eaten with rice or bread.

Classic Palestinian food, because it was rich, catered to special occasions. Examples are *snuniyya*, which is the special desert served when a child started teething, and *mughli*, served to the mother and guests after she gives birth to a child. There were certain kinds of drinks that were popular during Ramadan, like *qamar al-din*, made of dried apricots soaked in water and licorice extract. On 'Eid al-Fitr, stuffed lambs were eaten (by wealthier people), and *ma'mul* and *baqlawa* were popular sweets to serve to guests. On Easter, in addition to colored boiled eggs, *ma'mul* and *ka'k*, both stuffed with dates or crushed walnuts mixed with sugar, are eaten. *Ka'k*, which is the shape of a small wheel, is symbolic of the crown of thorns that was placed on Jesus' head. *Ma'mul* is a symbol of the sponge that was dipped in vinegar with which Jesus Christ wetted his tongue when he was on the cross. Colored eggs are a symbol of the Resurrection. In fact, there was always a special kind of food and/or sweet made for each occasion.

On the first day of the year, Christians eat *kunafa* with cheese and offer their guests *kunafa* with walnuts. In addition they cook seven kinds of food, symbolic of the seven good years. One of these is *labaniyya*, a dish cooked with yogurt, for its white color, and the other is *mulukhiyya*, for its green color.

Unfortunately, these good old days have given way to a modern life that is characterized by fast and materialistic trends. However, some people still value these traditions and observe them.

16.
Death

"… and have appointed for them an end whereof there is no doubt."

EVERYTHING HAS A START AS WELL AS AN END. Such is man's life; it starts as an embryo in a womb and ends with death.

From time immemorial, man has endeavored to understand the secret of existence and tried to find the way to immortal life. Most legends of the past have details of heroic adventures with the purpose of finding a tree, an herb, or a drink that might grant man immortality. In Arabic culture, there are expressions that people repeat on various occasions that express a wish for a longer life. For example, one may request something from someone else and say, "may you have a long life!", an expression that stands for "please." When a person buys new clothes, a friend will wish they live long enough to wear them out. Many religions, from the time of the ancient Egyptians, perhaps as a kind of resistance to the idea of death, believe in another life after death.

At the beginning of the 20th century, the death of the head of the family was a great disaster, especially after the people of Jerusalem and the whole region suffered from the tragic consequences of *safarbarlek*. This was a Turkish expression that signified the travel of young men conscripted by the Ottomans to fight in distant and unknown places during the First World War. Most of those young men never returned, leaving their families in poverty. This gave rise to the practice of young men marrying their brothers' widows for the purpose of taking care of them and their children. If the dead man's brothers were financially unable to support the family, the widow would have to find a job that suited her qualifications. Some orphaned children also had to find low-income work. Orphanages and schools could sometimes help fatherless children. In 1921, the High Islamic Council established the Islamic Orphanage School in Jerusalem, and many orphans were enrolled. Later they graduated as skilled laborers in such trades as carpentry, blacksmithing, and others.

The average life expectancy at the beginning of the 20th century was as low as 45 years, due to the prevalence of disease and epidemics as a result of poverty and malnutrition. The death rate, particularly among children, was very high. By the end of the century, however, with an increase in the standard of living, increased education, and better health care, life expectancy had increased to 60 years, on average.

Faithful believers would ascribe death, which they believed to be the natural end of life, as subject to the direct will of God. With the low standard of medicine in the old days and the general ignorance of people in health matters, the direct reason of death was mostly described in generalized terms. For instance, typhoid was described as "fever in the abdomen," and was an illness that had a fatal prognosis before the discovery of antibiotics. Chronic diseases, like cancer, diabetes, and high blood pressure, were unknown to people at that time.

People suffered the tragedy of death, whether it was sudden or after a long struggle with illness. Part of the tragedy in sudden death was that the patient's family was taken by surprise and unprepared; if this was the case the family might suffer financially and psychologically. If death was expected, it would be prepared for; the deceased person would have had time to see beloved family members, grant them forgiveness, and give the children necessary information about important worldly matters. One of the old customs was to lay the dying person in such a way so that they faced the direction of Mecca. People believed that the human soul left the body through the mouth. That is why people were careful to wet the patient's mouth with water, as a means of facilitating easy departure of the soul.

Before the appearance of modern media, death was announced by word of mouth. If some of the relatives of the deceased were living abroad or in another town, the news was given to a traveler to pass it to the relatives concerned. At the moment of death, especially if the deceased was still young or death occurred suddenly, women could be heard crying at the top of their voices, repeating phrases that would express their feeling of tragedy. Some of them would be caught by a fit of hysteria, tearing their clothes and beating themselves on the face and chest. Other women would try to calm down the hysterical woman by caressing her while reading verses from the Holy Book. It was expected that a widow with no children would have a stronger feeling of bitterness at the death of her husband, for she would feel lonely and people would think of her as having been unable to give her husband children bearing his name.

Relatives, neighbors, and friends showed their emotions and offered their help in a way that would make preparations for the funeral easier. Within a few hours, when the first shock had been absorbed, the family, with the help of relatives and neighbors, would start preparing for the funeral procession. Until the time of the British Mandate, certificates of death from doctors were not necessary. It was the *mukhtar*, the man chosen to take care of civil affairs in the quarter or the village, who would be the first to be informed about the death and would tacitly approve the burial.

Part of the preparation for the funeral consisted of washing the body of the dead person and wrapping it in a white shroud. This was done by a team of men or women who specialized in preparing the body for proper burial. If the dead man was married to two women, his body was washed twice. After the washing, the deceased was carried in a covered wooden coffin. In Islam it is believed that fast burial of the dead shows respect. That is why burial takes place as soon as possible. Some people buried the dead body with some verses from the Holy Book, together with a piece of paper in a bottle certifying that he or she was a faithful person. In the past, people believed that this paper would put the dead person at ease in the desolation of the grave.

People have always believed that offering a hand in carrying the dead to the grave is a source of blessing. At the funeral, the family members of the dead person walked right behind the coffin, taking turns carrying it, until the funeral reached al-Aqsa Mosque, where the funeral prayer was performed after the official prayers of *Dhuhr* (noon) or *'Asr* (afternoon). After that, the coffin was carried in the funeral procession to the graveyard.

If the deceased was a prominent figure in society, a musical band would accompany the funeral and play mourning tunes. If the deceased was a martyr, the coffin would be carried without its cover, or the martyr would be carried on a stretcher or directly over people's arms. This scene has been repeated after the Israeli occupation of Jerusalem, especially after the intifada. Funerals of martyrs always take the shape of protest demonstrations to challenge the occupation, and usually end with a violent encounter with the occupying army.

It is important to mention here that women in Jerusalem never took part in the funeral procession, and did not go to the graveyard until the funeral service was over.

Funeral processions in the past, when the city was small, used to be on foot. Nowadays, as the city has grown in width and length and distances have become too long to be walked, the deceased is carried in an ambulance or in a special funeral car, followed by other cars forming the funeral procession. One of the old customs that was possible when the city was small was passing in front of the deceased person's house before the funeral proceeded to the graveyard. The idea was to give the deceased "the last look" at his or her house. This luxury is no longer possible in a vast city. A lucky person was one whose death occurred on a Friday, especially "orphan Friday," the last Friday of Ramadan. It was believed that this was a sign of God's blessings.

In the old days when the funeral procession was on foot, participants used to repeat the name of God, *"La ilah ila Allah"* (No god but God!) during the processions. When complete silence prevailed, a voice would be heard saying, *"wahhiduh!"* (proclaim His oneness) and people would repeat the phrase, "No god but God!"

There was a custom in the villages, but never in Jerusalem, that at the moment the body of a dead woman was placed in the grave, her widower would step into the grave and demand a promise from her father or brothers to be engaged to her sister or one of their daughters. In some special cases, a woman might do the opposite when her dead husband was about to be buried. She would get into the grave and demand a promise not to be married to another man if she wanted to stay with her children at her late husband's house. She might also do the same to announce her pregnancy from her late husband, so that people of the village would be witnesses to her case. The origin of the custom of women demanding to remain with their children rather than getting married again goes back to the fact some people were inclined to have their young daughters get married soon after they lost their husbands in order to protect their honorable reputations.

The closest relatives of the deceased would lay the body in the grave. If the deceased was a woman who had no children or relatives, a man would announce his brotherhood to her in front of God, and take care of laying her body in the grave. It is an Islamic habit that the dead body is laid in the grave facing Mecca.

When the burial was concluded, a stone, called *shahed*, was placed at the head of the dead body until a gravestone was built, the size of which would be according to the financial abilities of the family. After verses from the Holy Qur'an were read, people shook hands with family members of the deceased, offering their condolences and wishing them God's blessings. Then everybody would leave the graveyard, which was the end of the funeral procession. It is important to mention that when death occurred, all people were obliged to offer their condolences to the family of the deceased. This was an occasion for people with enmity to forgive each other.

The custom was for the family of the deceased to serve lunch to the people coming from outside the city. Since the family of the dead would have no time to prepare food, relatives, friends, and neighbors would take care of this task. This was an old expression of social cooperation among people. People who could not take part in the preparation of food usually sent contributions, like a bag of rice, sugar, or coffee.

At the house of one of the family members, condolences would be received for three days. Arab bitter coffee was served, and verses from the Holy Qur'an were read by a specialized reader. Men were received in one place and women in another.

Under Israeli occupation, paying condolences has become a suitable occasion for people to gather together and to show their opposition to the occupying authorities, since political and social gatherings are prohibited. The political situation and social conditions are the preferred topics of discussion.

Naturally, when people sit together, they speak to each other. However, when the reader of the Holy Qur'an started his reading, silence would prevail and people could not leave until the reader had finished reading. On the third day of the condolences, the whole Qur'an would be read by a few people, each silently reading a part of the Holy Book. In the old days, after the readings were done, attendants were served supper. Nowadays only *kunafa* is offered. Muslims have special respect for Mondays and Thursdays. On these two days, the family of the dead person would usually give away food and money to the poor as a good omen for the dead person's soul. For the entire first year after a person's death, on Thursdays women would visit the grave, where they read verses of the Qur'an dedicated to the soul of the dead person. For the first three consecutive weeks, the whole Qur'an would be read on Thursdays at home, where relatives and friends take part. The same would be done on the fortieth day after death.

Women, who usually received condolences in the morning until noon, would be more emotionally effusive. The day after burial, female members of the family would visit the grave where they cried and prayed and gave away food to the poor. Christian women would light incense at the grave.

If the deceased was a martyr, with the certainty that he or she was chosen by God for Heaven, the family would receive felicitations, not condolences, and instead of women crying, they loudly utter *zagharid*. The martyr's family members, in spite of their inner feeling of sorrow, showed their pride. This deep faith in martyrdom was what made people willing to fight against the occupying forces with great courage. In fact, this faith and steadfast attitude is a source of great worry for the Israelis.

Particularly in the old days, in spite of the fact that mourning is unacceptable in Islam, when a dear person fell dead, men of his immediate family used to take off their *'iqal* (traditional Arab headdress) and refrain from bathing, shaving, or taking off their clothes for 15 to 40 days. Women used to put mud and soot on their faces, wear black clothes, and refrain from washing their body and wearing jewelry for 40 days. After the lapse of 40 days, female friends would urge women to go back to their normal life. Usually the dead person's widow and mother kept mourning for a longer time. The mother may mourn forever, but the widow for two years. A widow may not leave the family house except after the lapse of *'idda*, which is 130 days after the death of her husband, as this assures that, if she was pregnant, it was her husband who was the father.

Nowadays, many of these customs have been abandoned, partly because they do not suit modern life and partly because, according to the specialists in Islamic law, all these habits are considered *bida'* (novelties) and have nothing to do with Islam. In Palestine, the high number of martyrs has made death commonplace and more accepted.

Nowadays, the announcement of death is easily done through newspapers. This, unfortunately, has become more a matter of ostentation than a sincere intention to advise people of the death. It has also given rise to another unacceptable behavior, that of paying condolences by advertising in the newspapers. The size of the advertisement, whether that of the deceased's family or of those paying their condolences, has become a way to show off the financial ability of the family.

As far as Christians are concerned, they differ from Muslims in that when the relatives of a sick person feel that he or she is about to die, they call the priest, who comes to bless the dying and perform the necessary religious rituals. This includes confession in certain cases, if the dying person is able to do so. Repetition of the priest's visits indicates that the patient is in critical condition and the expression of sorrow would be the same as with Muslims. Informing the relatives of the event and the preparations for the funeral procession would take the same course.

However, Christians have different funeral customs. Instead of wrapping the dead person in a white shroud, they dressed them in their best clothes, and left the wedding ring on the person's finger. In addition, candles would be lit and flowers placed around the coffin. The body of the deceased would remain at home until the time of the funeral procession.

Coffins used by Christians are heavy. Therefore, instead of being carried by men, they were carried on a cart drawn by horses. The funeral cart was black with a cross on its top and driven by a coachman dressed in suitable clothes. Nowadays, a special black motorcar is used in lieu of the cart.

The coffin is followed by a team of scouts, carriers of flower wreathes, and the relatives of the deceased, both men and women, together with friends, clergy, and city notables. At the church, prayers and other rituals are performed; the dead is then taken to the grave, where the whole coffin is lowered into the grave and buried. After burial, family members receive condolences in the same manner as Muslims. Special food, either flour or wheat boiled with sugar, is given away to the poor; the same thing is repeated on the ninth day after death, on the 40th day, after half a year and after one year, as well as on Sundays and feasts.

My knowledge of Jewish funeral traditions is too limited for me to discuss fully here. As a native Jerusalemite, my relationship with the Jews in Palestine, most of whom were of European origin, was almost zero. What I remember is that they carried their dead on a stretcher and burrried the body at the Jewish graveyard at Ras al-'Amud, which is a piece of land rented from the Islamic Awqaf for 99 years. (This lease has already come to an end and has not been renewed.) We were told that should a Muslim or Christian pass below the stretcher, the dead body would be left on the ground, for they believed that it would have become impure. They would lift it again only if the same person passed below it from the opposite direction.

In all cases, after the formalities of the funeral and the condolences, relatives of the deceased would go to the court where the inheritance would be calculated and divided among the heirs. In many cases, this division of the inheritance was likely to give rise to family differences that simply increased their sorrows. When the deceased was a woman, her jewelry, if any, would also give rise to differences, like whether it was to be divided among all her heirs or taken only by her daughters.

CHAPTER SIXTEEN: DEATH

Olive picking

Conclusion

HE WHO DOES NOT LOVE HIS HOMELAND does not love life. This kind of love is particularly felt when one is far away from one's homeland. Its memory, saturated with the scent of history, remains deep in the heart. It is remembered as a line of events moving one after the other and filling one's heart with great happiness; happiness because one's homeland has been brought to one's heart.

So it was!

This book represents a tableau of political, human, artistic, and cultural scenes, as well as scenes of our struggle for freedom and against colonial settlement; scenes related to my life in my holy city of Jerusalem, whose history goes back thousands of years, the city on which our Arab-Canaanite forefathers left their fingerprints that will remain forever.

These events represent the continuity of history as it passes from parent to child, crystallizing habits and traditions that have characterized the people of Jerusalem. Their most important character was their deep belief in God, which in turn led to good human and ethical habits. In addition to being keen on performing religious rituals, they had good social habits derived from religious belief. Examples are good relations among members of the family, neighbors, and the whole society; respect shown by the young to the old; cooperation; and special care given to women relatives, even if married and living away from their original homes, a habit rarely found in the norms of other societies. Social cooperation has always been a tacit norm that urged society members to support the poor members of their society, especially on important happy and sad occasions. Taking good care of one's neighbor, to the extent of treating them as a member of the family, is another pillar of our traditions. Add to that the customs relating to food and beverages and cleanliness of the body and household.

Regarding education, people have always adhered to the old Arab saying, "Go for learning from the cradle to the grave." Learning has always been encouraged and led to a widespread and high respect for education, to the extent of considering it an almost sacred task.

Jerusalem has had special traditions for various pleasant events, such as the birth of a new child, the circumcision of a Muslim boy, the baptism of a newborn Christian child, or celebrating new marriages. The celebrations were simple, and cooperation among society members were demonstrated in these occasions. Relatives and friends usually offered *nuqut*, which is an amount of money or a gift of something necessary for the occasion, the idea being to help the celebrating family bear the expenses of the occasion. This was considered a kind of debt that was returned when the *nuqut* giver had a similar event in the future. In these celebrations, popular arts of dancing and singing, as well as special types of traditional foods were enjoyed.

While the systematic campaign of Zionist terrorism against Jerusalem is being blatantly performed, one remembers the popular festivals that characterized Jerusalem, like the festival of al-Nabi Musa (Prophet Moses), which demonstrated the national spirit and the struggle for freedom.

For every start there is an end. The day must come when a person's life comes to an end. Happy is he whose life comes to an end in the soil of his homeland.

Notes

1 Keith W. Whitelam, *The Invention of Ancient Israel* (London: Routledge, 1997) pp. 2–3

2 Wassef Jawhariyya, Revised and edited by Salim Tamari, *Majallat al-Dirasat al-Filastiniyya, Journal of Palestine Studies*, No. 44 (Autumn 2000)

3 Rabiha Dajani Miqdadi, *Rihlati ma' al-'Umr* [The Journey of My Life] (Beirut, 2000) p. 34

4 We must not forget that the relationship between Arab Jews and the rest of the Palestinians, both Muslim and Christian, was normally good. It was the large-scale immigration by European Jews that spoiled this atmosphere of peaceful coexistence.

5 Akka is on the coast of northern Palestine and Arwad is an island off the coast of Syria.

6 The Jerusalem ID allows the holder to enter and live in Jerusalem and Israel. The Israeli government has increasingly tried to withdraw Jerusalem ID cards from any Jerusalemite who cannot show that "the center of their life" is in Jerusalem, e.g. if they live outside the municipal boundaries. With a West Bank ID card, a Palestinian may no longer enter Jerusalem without special authorization from the Israeli authorities.

7 Antar of Abs was a great pre-Islamic hero who belonged to the tribe of Abs.

8 Victor Sahhab, *Traditions, Beliefs and Popular Crafts in Pre-1948 Palestine* (Beirut: Dar al-Hamra, 1993) p.46

9 These are the names of the two sons of Ali ibn Abi-Taleb, the fourth Islamic Caliph and cousin and son-in-law of the Prophet Muhammad. He and his sons, the grandsons of the Prophet, are especially respected by Shiite Muslims.

10 Halima al-Sadiyya was the infant Muhammad's nursemaid.

11 Zamzam Well is a spring of water that, according to religious fable, gushed out of the ground in Mecca when Abraham asked God to provide water for him and his people in that barren valley. God ordered Abraham to stamp the ground strongly with his feet. When he did so, water gushed out, and still does to this day.

12 Medina, the second Muslim holy city in the Holy Land of Hijaz, had the name of Yathrab before Islam. When the Prophet Muhammad was give asylum there, it was called al-Madina 'l-Munawwara (the enlightened city), abbreviated to Medina.

13 Keith W. Whitelam, *The Invention of Ancient Israel* (London: Routledge, 1997) p. 3

14 International opinion, like the three monkeys, has developed the same habits: see nothing, hear nothing, speak nothing.

Glossary

'amoura: female demon
arak: alcoholic drink made of aniseed
'Askalan: Ashkalon

bab: door, gate
Bab al-'Amud: Damascus Gate
Bab al-Asbat: Lion's Gate
Bab Hutta: neighborhood of the Old City, north of the al-Aqsa Mosque precinct
baqlawa: traditional sweet pastry in the Middle East and Asia
barjis: traditional board game played by women
bayraq: Turkish flag
bishara: money or cloth paid when a baby boy is born

dabka: traditional stamping dance from greater Syria
darwish (pl. *darawish*): Sufi follower

'Eid: feast, festival
'Eid al-Adha: feast of sacrifice
'Eid al-Fitr: feast of breaking the fast at the end of Ramadan
'eidiyya: gift on the occasion of the 'Eid

faqih: jurist
al-Fatiha: opening sura of the Qur'an

ghoul: demon

hajj: pilgrimage
hakawati: traditional story teller
hawsh: courtyard or cluster of houses around an alley
hijriyya, *hijri year*: year according to the Islamic (lunar) calendar

imam: prayer leader in the Mosque
'imama: turban

jaha: delegation of respected men who would go to ask for a girl's hand in marriage from her male relatives
jamid: dried yogurt
jinn, *jinni*: genie, spirit, or demon
jizya: tax on free non-Muslims living under Muslim rule

jum'a: Friday
al-Jum'a 'l-yatima: literally "orphan Friday," the last Friday in Ramadan

khatib: preacher in the Mosque
kufiyya: checked cloth covering for a man's head
kunafa: sweet made with finely spun, crisp pastry, cream, or cheese and nuts

ma'dhun: sheikh authorized to perform marriages
ma'mul: date or walnut-filled cakes made for 'Eid
mansaf: dish of rice and mutton
mashrabiyya: wooden blinds used to cover windows; women would peer out through them to see passers by
al-Mascobiyya: Russian Quarter of Jerusalem; now the name of a detention center in the quarter
mezze: light dishes, served before or instead of a meal
Mishnah (Jewish): Rabbinic compilation of traditions dating from 70–200 AD
mujahideen: resistance fighters, literally means strugglers
mufti: chief theologian with right to deliver legal opinions
mughli: sweet cooked with semolina, honey, and nuts
musakhkhan: dish of chicken and fried onions on bread
musta'rabin: As it appears here it means those who pretend to be Arabs, informers dressed like Arabs. In other cases, *musta'rabin* means those who learn Arabic or non-Arabs who speak it.
muwwal: a traditional genre of vocal music that is usually presented as a prelude before the actual song begins. It is characterized by making vowel syllables longer than usual.

nabi: Prophet
al-Nabi Musa: the Prophet Moses
najasah: impurity
nargile: water pipe, shisha

qarina: female demon
qatayef: dessert filled with cheese or nuts, coated with syrup, and cooked in melted butter
qawwas: bowmen

Ras al-'Amud: Damascus Gate of Jerusalem's Old City

sabil: fountain, place with water for passers by
saj: thin bread cooked on a griddle

saqqa': person who carries water
sheikh: leader, chief, old man, elder
sharif, (pl. *ashraf*): descendent of the Prophet Muhammad
silat al-rahm: upholding the ties of kinship by visiting female relatives that have married and live in other homes
shrak: thin whole-wheat bread cooked on a griddle
Sufi: Muslim mystic
souq: market
sura: chapter of the Qur'an

tabliyya: low table
tabun: traditional clay oven shaped like a half-cone
Tarawih: Ramadan prayers during which the Qur'an is recited over several nights
tarbush: fez
tariqa: Sufi way, Sufi religious order

wahma: birthmark
waqf (pl. *awqaf*): religious endowment

'ulama: men learned in religion

zaffa: wedding procession
zahgruda (pl. *zagharid*): ululations
zawiya (pl. *zawaya*): closed place, corner, Sufi school